PSYCHODRAMA

Paul Wilkins

SAGE Publications
London • Thousand Oaks • New Delhi

SAGE Publications Ltd
6 Bonhill Street
London EC2A 4PU

SAGE Publications Inc
2455 Teller Road
Thousand Oaks, California 91320

SAGE Publications India Pvt Ltd
32, M-Block Market
Greater Kailash – I
New Delhi 110 048

British Library Cataloguing in Publication data

A catalogue record for this book is
available from the British Library

ISBN 0–7619–5702–2
ISBN 0–7619–5703–0 (pbk)

Library of Congress catalog card number 99-72924

Typeset by Photoprint, Torquay, Devon
Printed in Great Britain by Biddles Ltd, Guildford, Surrey

To my father, Alfred Wilkins

CONTENTS

Author's Preface

Psychodrama is an action method of psychotherapy which has a distinctive language and a characteristic structure. In telling the story of this approach, I have used this language and this structure to give shape and form to my book. The way the chapters are arranged and titled loosely reflects the way psychodrama may be thought about and implemented. Broadly speaking (with the exception of the first and last chapters which deal with the building blocks from which psychodrama developed and the critical evaluation of psychodrama respectively), the chapter headings follow the shape of a typical psychodrama session. Just as before psychodrama can happen the place for it to do so must be established, so chapter 2 (Setting the Stage) deals with the ideas and techniques fundamental to the practice of psychodrama. The third chapter reflects the 'warm-up' which, in a psychodrama session is a necessary precursor to action. In a similar way, chapter 3 deals with the elements necessary to prepare a psychodramatist for practice. Chapter 4 reflects the scene-setting stage of a psychodrama in which the protagonist (or person who is the key player in the enactment) works with the director, using props and sometimes people to establish on the psychodrama 'stage' the physical environment which is the setting for the ensuing enactment. This chapter deals with the ways in which a group may be introduced to the psychodramatic form.

A traditional psychodrama is said to comprise at least three scenes. Accordingly, chapters 5, 6 and 7 are headed 'The First Scene', 'The Second Scene' and 'The Third Scene' respectively. Chapter 5 deals with the process of encounter, psychodramatic warm-ups and the way in which a protagonist may be identified and a director chosen. It also shows how the protagonist and the director establish a scene and how members of the group take roles in a developing enactment. Chapter 6 deals with the way in which a psychodrama enactment progresses through a number of scenes until some kind of end point is reached. Chapter 7 deals with the elements which complete a psychodrama session including 'sharing' (the process of reconnecting the protagonist with the group as group members tell of the feelings and experiences they share with the protagonist) and with closure.

Chapter 8 is headed 'Sharing' and in it I 'share' something of what I know about the professional contexts of psychodrama, describing the supporting infrastructure of the approach, the availability of training, employment as a psychodramatist, joining a psychodrama group and how to find out more about psychodrama. As mentioned above, Chapter 9 provides a critical look at psychodrama. The heading 'Processing' is an analogy with the final element of a psychodrama training session in which the work of student directors is critically evaluated by trainers and peers. In this chapter, I deal with psychodrama research and resistance to and criticisms of psychodrama.

ACKNOWLEDGEMENTS

My thanks go to Jenny Biancardi, from whom I have learnt so much, and to Marcia Karp, without whom psychodrama in the United Kingdom, if it was practised at all, would be much less than it is. They have both been essential to the genesis of this book. Thank you too to my friends Jan Costa and Frances McDonnell, who read the manuscript in draft. Lastly, I would like to thank everybody who contributed to my growth as a psychodrama psychotherapist, including my colleagues in the British Psychodrama Association and fellow members of my psychodrama training group. My special thanks go to Nadine Littledale, Maria Lumsden and Ben Smith.

1

LOCUS, MATRIX AND STATUS NASCENDI: THE BIRTH OF PSYCHODRAMA

Note

The language of psychodrama contains many unusual terms. This is less an attempt to baffle the uninitiated with jargon and more about being 'precise'. Some of these words reflect the theatrical origins of psychodrama, some arose because there was no existing word to convey the exact meaning, and some came from the education and background of J.L. Moreno, the founder of the approach. These terms are usually defined in the text of this book (although not necessarily where they first occur), but readers may find the glossary of psychodrama terms in Appendix 1 helpful. Where words defined in the glossary first appear in the text, they are written in a distinctive typeface *thus*.

Case Material

Because my aim has been in part to adopt the psycho-drama instruction 'Don't tell us, show us', throughout the

book, you will find examples and illustrations from practice. These are in italic type. Although they are drawn from
actual practice, each of these 'case histories' has been
disguised or fictionalized in some way. Names, locations,
detail and content are altered but the process is as given.

In psychodrama, scenes from the past, present or future, real or
imagined, are enacted to facilitate growth and healing.

(From the promotional literature for a psychodrama group)

This book tells the story of psychodrama, which is a particularly
potent approach to psychotherapy. The tale of psychodrama is
also the tale of the people who have been party to its creation,
development and continuing spread around the world. First of
these is Jacob Levy Moreno (1889–1974) from whose colourful life,
experiences and unorthodox approach psychodrama and its associated disciplines sprang. Perhaps, in the terminology of psychodrama, Moreno is the *protagonist* in this story, but many other
people play roles in it – each of them is an *auxiliary* in this tale
(and of course a protagonist in their own sub-plot).

Zerka Moreno was Moreno's partner in his later years and
collaborated with him in the production of some of the classic
psychodrama texts. She is still actively contributing to the theory
and practice of psychodrama at the start of her ninth decade.
Adam Blatner is also an important American psychodramatist and
has written significant psychodrama texts (see, for example, Blatner, 1971, 1997 and Blatner with Blatner, 1988). Anne Schutzenberger (1991: 203–224) took what she had learned from Moreno back
to France and (among other things) combined this knowledge with
some of the thinking from the analytic tradition in her work with
cancer patients.

Although there had been some previous effort in this direction
(Dean and Doreen Elephery had been running a training group two
or three times a year and Moreno himself had given a demonstration at the Maudsley Hospital, London in the 1940s), Marcia Karp
(1988: 45–50) was largely responsible for bringing psychodrama
and psychodrama training to Britain. Max Clayton (1988: 66)
credits Heather McLean as playing a large part in the development
of psychodrama in Australia and New Zealand and has helped that

region to become a stronghold of sociodrama. South America also features prominently on the psychodrama stage (there are reputed to be more psychodramatists in Brazil than in any other country) and, among others, Dalmiro Bustos and Monica Zuretti (both from Argentina) have made significant contributions. June Hare (1988: 51–58) wrote about psychodrama in Israel, where Peter Felix Kellerman is another significant figure. He was one of the key figures behind the international conference for psychodrama held in Jerusalem in 1996. In continental Europe, Dag Blomkvist in Sweden and Martti Lindqvist in Finland are to be included as senior figures.

Other psychodramatists have taken on the role of combining Moreno's ideas and practices with those from other areas of psychotherapy. Paul Holmes (1992) has written about object relations theory and psychodrama, while Aronson (1991: 199–203) integrates psychodrama and psychoanalytic group therapy. Anthony Williams (1991) writes of a combination of systems theory and dramatic action and Jenny Biancardi has done much to promote the practice of psychodrama from a person-centred perspective (see Wilkins, 1994a, 1994b).

Each of these (and those mentioned elsewhere in this book) has contributed and continues to contribute to the development of psychodrama. The story of psychodrama is their story. It is also the story of everybody who has ever written about, directed or participated in psychodrama, which is nothing without the spontaneity and creativity of its practitioners, theorists and participants.

What is Psychodrama?

What some psychodramatists say:

> [Psychodrama] is a form of group psychotherapy in which action techniques are used. Group members do not sit in a circle on chairs discussing life and its problems. Life is brought into the room and enacted using group members as the cast of the drama. The process is rich, enlivening and fun. Solutions are found to problems using the creativity and spontaneity of the group. (Holmes, 1992: 6–7)

> [In psychodrama] the action that takes place in a group is a way of looking at one's life as it moves. It is a way of looking at what happened and what didn't happen in a given situation. All scenes take place in the present, even though a person may want to enact something from the past or something in the future. The group enacts a portion of life as if on a video seen through the eyes of the protagonist or subject of the session. (Karp, 1995: 294)

Psychodrama is a group approach to psychotherapy and so the protagonist is not only in relationship with the facilitator but *with every other member of the group*. This provides a prodigious force for therapeutic change and healing. (Wilkins, 1994b: 44, original emphasis)

The aim of psychodrama is to help a person be more constructively spontaneous, be happier and have the strength to design life as she wants it to be. The objectives of insight and cathartic release play their part in unblocking the person's perception and ability to deal with change. Jan Costa (personal communication, 1995)

What the clients say:

'Psychodrama is a very powerful way of working.'
'Psychodrama was for me an enriching and powerful experience.'

These are the views of two members of a psychodrama group as the group came to an end.

Kellerman (1992: 17–18) points out that Moreno defined psychodrama differently at different times and in different contexts. These definitions include 'a theology with religious postulations', 'a dramatic art form with ascetic ideals', 'a political system with social values', 'a science with research ambitions', 'a method of psychotherapy with curative goals' and 'a philosophy of life'. Kellerman proposes that psychodrama should be viewed 'as a specific method of psychotherapy, a treatment approach to psychological problems'. He (1992: 11–12) offers the following definition:

In psychodrama, participants are invited to re-enact significant experiences and to present their subjective worlds with the aid of a group. Every aspect of life can thus be re-enacted . . . Psychodramatic scenes portray predictable developmental life events or sudden crises, inner conflicts or entangling relationships. . . . all psychodramas share the one common element that makes them therapeutic: the presentation of personal truth in the protected world of make-believe as a way to master and cope vicariously with stressful life events in a creative and adaptive manner.

Certainly, psychodrama is best known and has made greatest impact as an approach to psychotherapy but I suspect that the time of some of the other ways in which Moreno saw his creation as facilitating life and living is yet to come. For example, psychodrama is already used as a research tool (see Hawkins, 1988: 60–78) and I am sure that as research with people and into personal and group experience continues to move away from the traditional, 'scientific' or positivistic model, psychodrama has every chance of coming into its own. Also, as well as a powerful method of psychotherapy, psychodrama is an appropriate form for personal growth and has strengths as a medium of education. With these qualifications, I am happy to accept Kellerman's notion of psychodrama.

Psychodrama then, is primarily an action method of psychotherapy and personal growth which relies upon the innate spontaneity and creativity of human beings for its effectiveness. Most commonly, psychodrama is a group therapy but it can be practised one-to-one. Members of a psychodrama group are not required to possess acting skills and while group members may be invited to take on a role, participating in the action is a matter of personal choice.

In a psychodrama group, the facilitator (or **director**) while having a responsibility to the group as a whole and to each individual it comprises, normally works with one person (the protagonist) to establish and develop a scene or series of scenes. The protagonist may use objects in the room and/or other members of the group (who therefore become auxiliaries) to represent people, places or things integral to the unfolding drama. Other people in the group (the **audience**) have the important and far from passive responsibility to watch the action. What is required of anyone wishing to become a member of a psychodrama group is a willingness to encounter themselves and others with the intention of growing as a person and supporting the growth of all.

There may be as much to be gained from witnessing a psychodrama as from participating in it. Jan Costa (personal communication, 1994), a psychodrama practitioner and trainer of considerable experience, spoke of the importance of the processes of giving testimony and bearing witness to the process of healing. By this she meant that it is important that protagonists have the opportunity to 'tell' their stories of trauma, pain and damage ('This is how it was for me') and that these are heard by others. One of the distinguishing characteristics of psychodrama is that these painful stories (and stories of joy, ecstasy, confusion, indecision and so on) are enacted rather than told. The familiar invitation of a psychodrama director is 'Don't tell us, show us', for the prime belief of psychodramatists is that 'actions speak louder than words'.

Jacob Levy Moreno

> I hope that it does not sound immodest, but as psychodrama happens to be my most personal creation, its cradle my own autobiography may throw further light upon its final delivery. (Moreno, 1985: 2)

In his chapter 'The Cradle of Psychodrama' (1985: 1–20) Moreno is clear that his personal story and the story of psychodrama are inextricably linked. This way of working was *his* invention, it was also the product of a time and a place (turn of the century Vienna) and perhaps a culture. In psychodrama theory, the concepts of **status nascendi, locus** and **matrix** have some importance. Moreno (1985: 25) wrote:

> The status nascendi, the locus, and the matrix. These represent different phases of the same process. There is no 'thing' without its locus, no locus without its status nascendi, and no status nascendi without its matrix. The locus of a flower, for instance, is in the bed where it grows into a flower, and not its place in a woman's hair. Its status nascendi is that of a growing thing as it springs from the seed. Its matrix is the fertile seed, itself.

Bustos (1994: 65) writes that Moreno uses these words in a 'creative' or 'sometimes capricious way' and regards this as confusing. However, he states that, in Moreno's sense:

> The term 'locus' determines the place where *something* was born. Status nascendi is then the temporal dimension, the moment in which it occurs. So, the term matrix designates that *something* in its maximum specificity. (p. 65, original emphasis)

In a sense, Moreno is the matrix from which sprang psychodrama and the places and times of his life its locus and status nascendi.

Jacob Levy Moreno was born in Bucharest on 14 May 1889 into a family of Sephardic Jewish descent. His biographer Marineau (1989: 12–18) writes about Moreno's early life and his relationship with his parents. In Moreno's early relationships and experiences can be detected the seeds from which grew his philosophy and the practice of psychodrama. For example, from the age of four-and-a-half he engaged in games in which he took the part of God, and he himself (1985: 3) attributes the form of the **stage** in classical psychodrama (as three tiers with a balcony) to these early experiences. Hare and Hare (1996: 1–25), in their record of the life of Moreno, record that Moreno's absorption with God persisted into his early adulthood. They write: 'One day he saw himself as a servant of God, the next as a replica of the Almighty, and even as God himself' (p. 5). They also record that throughout this time of testing and trying, Moreno 'remained convinced that action was more important than words, experience a better teacher than books' (p. 5). This belief was to form the cornerstone of Moreno's contribution to psychotherapy, education and the righting of social injustice.

Moreno was not a modest man and was fond of telling stories of his early experiences and of people he met. Some of these stories are in apparent conflict with how events are recalled by others: Hare and Hare (1996: 2) report that Moreno's account of his birth is somewhat more romantic than that of his mother, and Zerka Moreno refers to Moreno's 'homespun myths' (see Hare and Hare, 1996: 24). Moreno records (1985: 5–6) that, while working in the Psychiatric Clinic in Vienna University, he attended a lecture given by Sigmund Freud. This lecture was Freud's analysis of a telepathic dream. Moreno writes of his one encounter with Freud:

> As the students filed out he asked me what I was doing. 'Well Dr Freud, I start where you leave off. You meet people in the artificial setting of your office, I meet them on the street and in their home, in their natural surroundings. You analyse their dreams. I try to give them the courage to dream again. *I teach the people how to play God.*' Dr Freud looked at me as if puzzled. (Moreno, 1985: 5–6, original emphasis)

Nothing is known of Freud's experience of this event and perhaps this is one of the 'homespun myths', but if it is, there is a sense in which it ought to be true. The more of Moreno's stories I encounter, the more I am impressed. They may not always be 'factual' but I think that they contain a quality of truth that supersedes mere actuality!

During his days as a medical student, Moreno continued his experiments with taking roles and exploring situations through enaction (by, for example, reconstructing trials of which he had witnessed the opening stages, playing all the significant participants and using his sense of role to forecast the outcome of the trial, a process which Marineau (1989: 40) indicates was often successful), but he was also beginning to develop in other ways.

Hare and Hare (1996: 8) state that Moreno gave the period 1913–14 as the 'genesis of group psychotherapy'. At this time, Moreno, with two colleagues, began to work with a group of prostitutes. As a result of this work, wrote Hare and Hare (1996: 9), 'Moreno began to see that one individual could become a therapeutic agent for another and the potentialities of a group psychotherapy on a reality level crystallized in his mind.' The two major threads which would constitute psychodrama (work in groups and the enacting of what was, what might be or what might have been) were thus beginning to be drawn together.

Other events contributed to the young Moreno's evolving philosophy. Hare and Hare (1996: 9–15) write of his experiences in the

First World War and in Vienna up until 1925. This period included the first great love affair of his life and his invention of 'spontaneity theatre'. Of the latter, Hare and Hare (1996: 13) write: 'groups of actors put on spontaneous plays in response to suggestions from the audience, and did re-enactments of the daily news in a "living newspaper," or improvised themes'.

The relationship of this form of drama with what Boal (1979) came to call 'Theatre of the Oppressed' and Playback Theatre as developed by Fox (1995) seems obvious. Nolte (1989: 131) refers to Moreno as a 'genius' whose thinking was 'ahead of the times' and 'truly novel'. Perhaps this is an example.

In 1925, for a variety of reasons (see Marineau, 1989: 94–99), Moreno left Austria for the United States. Here he eventually met and married Zerka Toeman (who as Zerka Moreno became his collaborator and a psychodrama practitioner and theorist of consequence herself) and established a private centre for psychodrama treatment and training at Beacon in New York State. He lived and worked at Beacon until his death in 1974.

Whatever has been added to or taken away from Moreno's ideas and practices by others, psychodrama remains the creation of one man. Hare and Hare (1996: 1) describe Moreno as 'a psychiatrist, dramatist, theologian, poet, philosopher, inventor, group psychologist, psychodramatist, sociodramatist, sociatrist, and educator'. They go on to say:

> Although he made significant contributions in all of these roles, the three areas in which he was most creative, and that have had a major impact on the theory and practice of social science and group psychotherapy are psychodrama, *sociodrama* and *sociometry*. For Moreno, each of these methods was a contribution to the overall process that would make it possible for men and women to realise their God-like creative potentials and thus fashion a world in which true liberation was possible. (p. 1)

From this, it would appear that Moreno was a visionary and that his work had an almost messianic flavour. Certainly, he (1985: 1) refers to the 'almost unlimited therapeutic potentialities which psychodrama has', and (in Moreno and Moreno, 1975: 11) he also wrote:

> The objective of psychodrama, was, from its inception, to construct a therapeutic setting which uses life as a model, to integrate into it all the modalities of living, beginning with the universals – time, space, reality,

and cosmos – down to all the details and nuances of life and reality practice.

Moreno's Core Concepts

To some extent, psychodramatists are divided as to the importance of the theoretical and philosophical ideas in practice. For many, these ideas are paramount. Others take the view that the techniques of psychodrama may be applied whatever the theoretical orientation of the practitioner. Thus there are psychodramatists who see themselves as practising in a psychoanalytic framework, those informed by the ideas of Rogers and so on. Blatner (1995: 2) considers that psychodrama is not a distinct philosophy but should be seen 'rather as a complement to an emerging, somewhat eclectic consensus', and Kellerman (1987a: 78) advanced the argument that 'psychodrama should be defined in a way that does not assume a theoretical orientation'. It is striking that psychodrama is so frequently defined as an action *method* of psychotherapy even by psychodramatists who consider themselves to take a traditional, Morenian view. This probably reflects and perpetuates the separation (real or artificial) between 'doing' psychodrama and the philosophy of Moreno.

The 'theory-free' view of psychodrama, the idea that it is a method or series of techniques which may be used from any psychotherapeutic or philosophical perspective, does not find universal acceptance. For example, Sprague (1994: 11–35) greatly values the underlying philosophy of psychodrama which he sees as holistic and (p. 12) as of particular 'relevance for us all as we approach the twenty-first century'. Bustos (1994: 64), who also sees psychodrama as having a distinct and important theoretical base, wrote of his initial difficulty in understanding his practice in terms of that theory. He attributes this to 'the chaos with which Moreno presented his thoughts'. Bustos suggests that to have produced a systematic, structured and complete doctrine was not in Moreno's nature and that the many contradictions in his words and writing 'left people free to order their own spontaneity'. This is both a strength and a weakness of psychodrama.

The great strength it brings is that psychodrama centres on action. It is experiential and its proponents learn by doing more than by reading or listening. In the course of psychodrama training, a student has many experiences in the roles of protagonist, auxiliary, group member and director. In this way, becoming a psychodramatist is a process of embodiment rather than intellectual learning alone. Theory, method and practice are one and the psychodramatist becomes integrated with philosophy in such a way as to scarcely realize it. This is a way of knowing described by Bohart (1996: 199–201) as experiencing. It is different from conceptual thinking in that it is 'primarily nonverbal, perceptual, holistic and gestalt-like, contextual, bodily and ecological'. Coming to really understand something is to 'get it at an experiential "gut level"'. The many attributes Bohart links to this way of knowing include 'the initial inspiration of creativity' and 'the important ecological skill [of detecting] patterns of meaning flowing over time, that is, to detect the trajectories in situations'. Creativity and the ability to know 'ecologically' are essential to the psychodrama practitioner. Perhaps something would be lost if psychodrama became codified and systematized in the way of some other psychotherapies?

Paradoxically, it is this emphasis on experiencing which leads to a lack of understanding of Moreno's ideas. Sprague (1994: 16) quotes Moreno thus:

> My philosophy has been misunderstood. It has been disregarded in many religious and scientific circles. This has not hindered me from continuing to develop techniques whereby my vision of what the world could be might be established in fact. It is curious that these techniques – sociometry, psychodrama, group therapy – created to implement an underlying philosophy of life have been almost universally accepted while the underlying philosophy has been relegated to the dark corners of library shelves or entirely pushed aside.

Nearly fifty years later, this remains true. But perhaps the picture is not quite as bleak as it seems. I believe that when I practise psychodrama from a person-centred perspective, I make use of core concepts drawn from the work and thought of Moreno. Just as Moreno's psychodrama is a vehicle I have chosen by which to implement person-centred philosophy and practice, so this in turn is a way of employing the thought of Moreno. I think that all psychodramatists, traditionalists, person-centred, systemic, group analytic therapists or whatever are in actuality true to Moreno's key concepts of *creativity* and *spontaneity* and that we invest great value in the process of *encounter*. These elements are fundamental to psychodrama theory. Moreno saw spontaneity and creativity as innate human qualities – Zerka Moreno (1989: 178) records that Moreno 'conceptualised that what is of essence in human experience are the twin principles of spontaneity and creativity'. Spontaneity is the wellspring of creativity and an objective of psychodrama is to enhance the spontaneity of the protagonist, the auxiliaries, the group and the director to bring about creative solution, resolution and/or release.

One definition of spontaneity Moreno (1953: 336) gave was 'a new response to an old situation or an adequate response to a new situation'. In this sense, an adequate response is one appropriate to circumstances 'with competency and skill' (Hare and Hare, 1996: 36). Spontaneity and anxiety are opposites. The more anxious a person is, the less spontaneous and therefore the less likely they are to meet challenge and change in a healthy way. In *Psychodrama*, Volume I (1985: 47–152), Moreno devotes over one hundred pages to 'The Principles of Spontaneity', which indicates its great importance. It is spontaneity which is the keystone of psychodrama. With creativity, it is a powerful innate force and the agent for change, healing and healthy living.

Spontaneity and creativity involve thinking, feeling, sensing, intuiting and doing and do not always manifest in spectacular fashion. In many ways, they are quite ordinary, playing a part in everyday events. Blatner with Blatner (1988: 64) in their chapter on spontaneity, wrote: 'Spontaneity need not be showy or dramatic; it can be unassuming. It can be present in the way you think, walk, look at nature, dance, or sing in the shower.' This is equally true of creativity.

Although spontaneity and creativity are universal human attributes, in many of us life events lead to them becoming blocked or distorted. Moreno's early thinking about spontaneity was to some extent triggered by watching children at play. Children's play involves a great deal of spontaneity – for example, the bringing of a freshness of mind to familiar objects so that a handful of beads becomes ranks of soldiers in dress uniform, a suburban garden becomes the entire Amazonian rain forest, full of strange plants and stranger creatures. Moreno noticed that as people grew older, so they seemed to become less spontaneous. This means that they are more prone to anxiety and less able to implement appropriate responses. In some circumstances, this can be so extreme as to cause disturbance, lack of well-being and ill-health. An explicit belief of psychodramatists is that rejuvenating or releasing blocked spontaneity and creativity leads to new solutions to old problems and better resources with which to meet new ones. This rejuvenation happens through the process of encounter.

Hare and Hare (1996: 36) state that 'encounter is the real basis of the psychotherapeutic process'. In the Morenian sense, encounter is the process of two people meeting face to face in the 'here-and-now'. In psychodrama psychotherapy, directors enter this encounter endeavouring to be present as themselves. In common with other humanistic therapies, the success of the therapeutic relationship depends upon the meeting of the real self of the therapist with the real self of the client. This reciprocity is an essential feature of encounter. The process of encounter can occur not only between the psychodrama director and the protagonist or other group member but also between any two individuals. This adds greatly to the power and efficacy of psychodrama. In this sense, psychodrama is a relationship-based psychotherapy because it relies on more than the technical skill of the director.

Through the process of encounter (and the application of psychodrama techniques) spontaneity and creativity are rejuvenated or enhanced. This leads to improved quality of life. It seems to me that, regardless of their professed orientation, each and every psychodramatist either explicitly or implicitly holds this to be true and practises accordingly. The exact form of that practice may differ, but in essence Moreno has provided the framework in which it can happen. Perhaps he would have been quite pleased to realize that his approach was in some ways big enough to contain so many others.

Uses of Psychodrama

In his introduction to the fourth edition of *Psychodrama*, Volume I, Moreno (1985: a) defines psychodrama 'as the science which explores the "truth" by dramatic methods'. This suggests that it is much more than a psychotherapy. Moreno and Moreno (1975: 270) say: 'Psychodrama can be exploratory, preventive, diagnostic, educational and psychiatric in its applications,' which indicates that psychodrama may function as a research tool and as a method of learning as well as a means of personal growth or psychotherapy.

The Uses and Settings of Psychodrama Psychotherapy
It is as an action method of psychotherapy that psychodrama is best known. Blatner with Blatner (1988: vii) offer the opinion that:

Psychodrama is unique among the psychotherapies in its capacity to address the widest range of issues: past, present, and future; intrapsychic, interpersonal, and group dynamics; support, education, expression, and insight; imagination and reality; emotions and cognition; spiritual, artistic, playful, and political aspects; prevention, diagnosis, and treatment; nonverbal communications; setting and props; and time for warming-up.

Rather more matter-of-factly, Karp (1995: 294) writing of psychodrama psychotherapy says:

Psychodrama has been defined as a way of practising living without being punished for making mistakes; that is to say, practising growing up while you are doing it. The action that takes place in a group is a way of looking at one's life as it moves.

Individually and together these quotations suggest that psychodrama is an enormously adaptable method. It may be applicable to many client groups and many settings. This is indeed the case. Hare and Hare (1996: 70) consider that the early work of Moreno 'foreshadowed' many of the current applications. They say, 'Moreno maintained that there was no classification of psychosis nor, indeed, any problems that are not amenable to treatment by psychodrama under certain conditions.' Kellerman (1992: 23) takes issue with this claim. He argues that, while

from one point of view, all people can benefit from psychodrama at various times in their life cycles, particularly when in emotional distress . . . [it] is my experience that, while a wide variety of people may benefit from psychodrama, others are simply unsuited either to psychodrama itself, or to the setting in which it is conducted.

In my experience, providing I am clear with them about what it involves, people generally know if psychodrama is right for them and I find it wisest to trust their instincts.

Psychodrama is used in clinical settings with people experiencing a wide variety of mental health difficulties, emotional predicaments or behavioural problems. For example, John Casson (personal communication, 1997) a psychodrama trainer and dramatherapist, uses psychodrama with people who hear voices and Honig (1991: 3–18) has written about using psychodrama with chronic schizophrenics. In the area of sexual abuse too psychodramatists have found uses for their skills. Bannister (1991: 7–93) has written about her work with sexually abused children and Karp (1991: 95–113) and Corti and Casson (1990: 37–53) describe their work with adults who were sexually abused. I have had some success in using psychodrama with people who consider them-selves to have an eating disorder and Jay (1992: 5–18) writes about her work with bulimic women. She says (p. 15):

> Women with bulimia often have difficulty in dealing with distressing feelings and resort to bingeing and vomiting as a way of dealing with them. Psychodrama can help the individual face the distress and teach her new skills in how to deal with the situation. It can also address underlying conflicts behind the bulimia in an environment that is supportive. Jane [a group member] went through a very difficult few weeks when her family were making unreasonable demands on her. Instead of eating she would bring the feelings to the group and was more able to share her distress with others as opposed to her usual pattern of isolated bingeing.

Psychodramatists work with problems of addiction. For exam-ple, Rustin and Olsson (1993: 12–22) describe their success with a particular psychodrama exercise they call the 'Sobriety Shop' and Ruscombe-King (1991: 155–177) tells the story of some of her work with alcoholics. She presents accounts of her work with four clients and discusses her attitude towards them. Of the process as a whole she says:

> It is difficult to predict whether the use of psychodrama with alcoholics as illustrated can influence drinking behaviour. I believe that the experience of psychodrama provides an opportunity for the rediscovery of personal potential common to every individual. In the alcoholic, that potential has been drowned by alcohol. The use of rediscovered poten-tial demands decisions and every individual retains the choice of returning to drink or of continuing to build on rediscoveries.

It isn't necessary to be 'ill' to benefit from psychodrama. Sprague (1991: 33–51) has written movingly of his work with young people with learning difficulties and psychodrama has been used success-fully in other settings with young people. For example, Özbay et al. (1993: 3–11) describe and evaluate their work with group members who had 'adjustment difficulties concerning adolescence along with a degree of identity confusion' (p. 5). In prisons too psycho-drama has found a role. Jefferies (1991: 189–200) worked with 'hard core offenders' and presents some case material. She quotes (p. 199) 'Tony', an inmate at Grendon prison, as saying (during a BBC Radio Four broadcast in 1985):

> What we are doing here is defusing bombs. What do you think you're gonna get from me if you put me in a cage for eight years and pump me with a stick; what do you think you're gonna get? You're gonna get me worse than when I came in and the same goes for everybody else. It's serious business, this. It quite annoys me actually when people say

psychodrama is a lot of cobblers. You should come with me for half an hour and I'll do one on you.

Jefferies herself says 'psychodrama has shown that it can change attitudes and behaviour; it offers a far more humane and constructive approach to the treatment of those convicted of serious crimes' (p. 199).

The list of the types of clients, settings and circumstances in which psychodrama has been and is being used is almost endless. Those described above represent just a few. It is primarily a group therapy but it can be used one-to-one (see, for example, Stein and Callahan, 1982: 118–129), it is used in institutional settings and in private practice and it has as big a part to play in personal growth as it does in addressing mental ill-health. Much of my own work is, for example, with people living 'normal' lives who wish to know more about psychodrama or who have the sense that psychodrama may be an aid to fuller and freer functioning. Members of my groups have included students, therapists, academics, actors, shop workers and administrators to name but a few. The work we have done together has ranged from the exploration of childhood trauma to the resolution of grief, from addressing self-doubt to explorations of potential. We have met and worked with sub-personalities of all kinds (see Wilkins, 1993: 5–17) and, psychodramatically, I have visited Provence for an evening meal, witnessed the dismemberment and burning of a beloved teddy bear in Eastern Europe, relaxed in the summer sunshine in rural Derbyshire while the protagonist told his friends how dear they were, been party to a scene of unbelievable desperation and desolation when news arrived of the death of a child, and so much more. I and my 'person in the street' clients are continually amazed at the richness and power of the techniques and processes of psychodrama and how helpful it can be.

Other Uses of Psychodrama
As important as the psychotherapeutic applications of psychodrama are, it would be mistaken to think of it as limited to that field. The role of psychodrama in education and supervision are of particular note, although all of these have as yet unfulfilled potential.

The most obvious use of psychodrama in 'education' is in the training of psychodramatists. Psychodrama training is essentially experiential and the training schemes approved by (for example) the British Psychodrama Association rely heavily upon the experience the trainee has in all roles in a psychodrama group. There is of course also considerable academic rigour and theoretical understanding must be demonstrated but there is a strongly held belief that the best way to understand psychodrama is to experience it. In a similar fashion, Costa and Walsh (1991: 24–37) chose to 'demystify' and demonstrate psychodrama for their colleagues in a psychiatric setting by offering them the opportunity to participate in a psychodrama group. Of this way of working, they say (p. 33) that group members are 'able to see the potential of this method for insight and growth'. And: 'It has been reported to us that material and issues worked on in the group have enabled members to review their clinical relationships from a deeper personal understanding.' In other words, the learning in this group was not just about psychodrama but that itself became the vehicle for an understanding of other areas of work.

In my own work as an educator, I use psychodrama in many ways. I find it a particularly useful way of demonstrating approaches to research to both students of psychodrama and undergraduates. Briefly, I encourage students to each take on a specified role and to 'become' that person for the duration of the exercise. We then use action to explore a number of ways in which the group might be understood in terms of these characteristics. These include quantitative and qualitative methods and empirical, hermeneutic and collaborative approaches.

The advantages of using psychodrama in the supervision of therapists are listed by VanderMay and Peake (1980: 30–31) and described in my own work (Wilkins, 1995: 256) thus:

> In supervision (as in therapy or personal growth), psychodrama offers a rich learning experience for the whole group. This is not only by demonstration but because it is truly a *group* process which may involve deeply not only those people in role and involved directly in the action but also those in the 'audience'. Through the medium of sharing, all members of the group can experience the supportive aspects of supervision (because they are communicating their personal experiences and these are being heard acceptingly and probably with empathy). Members of the audience may also become caught up in the experiential flow of the drama taking place before them and live it as if it were their own. This is a great deal more than a vicarious involvement – great personal understandings may be achieved.

Basically, in this context psychodrama is used to explore the client/therapist relationship offering the therapist (who becomes the protagonist) the opportunity to, for example, experience the inner world of the client through *role reversal*, explore strategies and the effect of possible interventions in *surplus reality* or to witness how other therapists in the group might deal with the client.

Sociodrama and Sociometry: the Social Atom of Psychodrama

Psychodrama is not the sole survivor of Moreno's prodigious work – it has its relatives and relationships, its *social atom*. Foremost amongst these are *sociodrama*, which is to social issues as psychodrama is to the personal, and *sociometry*, which is the 'science' of the measurement of interpersonal relationships. From these two, although receiving little attention at present, Moreno derived *sociatry*, which is the science of social healing and which is to group 'illness' what psychiatry is to individual illness (see Moreno, 1953: 379). Less well known variants of psychodrama include 'psychomusic' (see Moreno, 1985: 277–314).

Moreno (1953: 87) defined sociodrama as 'a deep action method dealing with intergroup relations and collective ideologies'. In outward form, psychodrama and sociodrama appear very similar but in the latter the focus is on a group working with an issue of social concern. For example, Goble (1990: 460–461) describes the use of sociodrama in psychiatric nurse training. The method was used to explore the issue of hospital violence and members of the group portrayed not only patients, nurses and doctors but also relatives, journalists and representatives of patient support groups. Goble (p. 460) writes: 'Sociodrama not only vividly highlighted how violent situations can and do arise at medication times, but also how such incidents can be prevented, particularly when patients' rights as individuals are respected.' Hare and Hare (1996: 59–63) present accounts of two sociodramas conducted by Moreno himself. The first of these deals with 'the black–white problem' and was conducted in the setting of an American university in 1945, the second is 'psychodrama and sociodrama of Judaism and the Eichmann trial' which took place in 1961. In both of these, Moreno involves the audience in an exploration of a potentially contentious issue of the day.

In recent years, sociodrama has not received the same attention as psychodrama and, apart from in Australia and New Zealand (where training in sociodrama has an honourable history), it seems to have become something of a 'poor relation'. Perhaps this is beginning to change. In the United Kingdom, sociodrama has been an important part of the work of Ken Sprague, and Ron Weiner has established the first British training in sociodrama in Leeds.

Sociometry 'has been a relatively obscure aspect of Moreno's work' (Blatner with Blatner, 1988: 137). Moreno considered socio-metry as being as important as psychodrama and much more than a way of measuring relationships in groups, which is a common succinct definition. Mendelson (1989: 138–139) picks up on this, defining sociometry thus:

> It can be thought of as a philosophy of life and as a philosophy for living, as a theory of man alone, and as a theory of men in groups (or a theory of society), as a methodology for exploring man and society and their interrelationships, and also as a therapeutic praxis that attempts to help man reach a higher level of personal humanity and interpersonal synergy.

He goes on to say 'a tradition of utilising sociometry in the midst of life itself is at the very heart of Moreno's original conception of sociometry'. In their important contribution to the understanding and use of sociometry, Carlson-Sabelli et al. (1994: 147) define sociometry as:

> a therapeutic intervention (not only an objective measurement), to promote personal choice, and to foster insight into the physical, bio-logical, social and psychological processes that predetermine them, and which may be largely outside the realm of free choice.

Like other members of the psychodrama family, sociometry is an action method, although it can also be a paper and pencil activity. Its techniques include the exploration of relationships between people by getting them to express their preferences for others in the group. This may take the form of an exercise such as asking each member of the group to place a hand on the shoulder of the person in the group whom (for example) they would find the most valuable companion on a desert island. Other choices might follow (ask for a loan, go to the cinema, share a confidence, eat lunch with and so on). This is a powerful way of establishing group cohesion and begins to demonstrate the complex web of relation-ships present in most groups. 'Sculpting' is another sociometric technique in which people are arranged in the available space in such a way as to demonstrate relationships. This is in terms of physical distance but, for example, posture may be an important element. Sculpting can be a way of modelling the group itself, either in relation to a particular person (perhaps the facilitator) or a concept (for example, psychodrama) or it may be a way of representing some of the 'outside' relationships of a group member.

Although it is sometimes used in the warm-up phase of psychodrama, like sociodrama and sociatry (at least in comparison to psychodrama), sociometry has to some extent fallen by the wayside. Blake and McCanse (1989: 148) record that reference to sociometry declined sharply through the 1970s and 1980s and they offer a rationale for the use of sociometry in industry. Carlson-Sabelli et al. (1994: 144–147) also make strong arguments for the use of sociometry.

2

SETTING THE STAGE: THE INSTRUMENTS AND TECHNIQUES OF PSYCHODRAMA

The Psychodrama Environment

Perhaps because of its kinship with the theatre, psychodrama has traditionally been practised on a 'stage'. This, Moreno (1953: 81) defined as 'the first instrument' of psychodrama. Marineau (1989: 81) says, 'Moreno always liked stages' and that he thought 'there was a need for a formal structure to support the therapeutic work'. The formal stage of Moreno, as used at his centre in Beacon, was three-tiered with a balcony, each step representing a different level of psychological involvement. An earlier stage design, developed around 1924 in Vienna, was circular, multilevel but lacked the balcony. In this model, the whole space was the stage. Marineau (1994: 91–92) considers that this type of stage 'reflected a philosophy in which everyone was equal and a participant'.

In the practice of psychodrama, the formality with which the stage is defined and circumscribed varies greatly. Very few psychodramatists now practise in a setting so structured as the Beacon theatre but descendants of both Morenian stages are to be found throughout the psychodrama world. Some practitioners who regularly work in the same space have an area of the room designated as a stage. This may be raised slightly above the level of the audience space and may even be equipped with theatre lighting.

Through the use of colour, spotlighting and so on, this can enhance, clarify or intensify the action:

> Certain scenes are made more vivid when enacted primarily under red light (e.g., hell, anger); amber light (e.g., a tawdry or sleazy event); blue light (e.g., introspective, heaven, dreamlike, depressed); relative darkness (e.g., shameful, intimate, isolated); green light (e.g., envious, deceitful), and so on. (Blatner with Blatner, 1988: 168)

This type of stage is the one most associated with classical Morenian psychodramatists. Even when they work in an otherwise ordinary room, psychodramatists who prefer this form will specify an area in which action may occur. This then becomes the stage. Karp (1995: 296) represents this view of the psychodrama stage when she says: 'Psychodrama which is attempted within the group space with no designated stage area, often falls flat because there are no boundaries spatially or methodologically.'

The other model – working in the round – is, according to Marineau (1994: 92–93) 'now widely used in psychoanalytic psychodrama'. It is also the preferred form in person-centred psychodrama. In my own practice, the protagonist chooses whereabouts in the room a scene will take place and the audience adjusts accordingly. Taking a different view to that of Karp, I (Wilkins 1994b: 45) offer the following rationale:

> Action takes place in any area of the group space designated by the protagonist and this is usually (but by no means always) 'in the round'. I prefer this approach to the use of a designated stage area because it allows the protagonist choice and flexibility. . . . This conveys an immediate message about control to the protagonist. It is her psychodrama and she decides where it takes place.

Because we sit together in a circle, and the action takes place in the middle of the group, this then acts as a symbolic holder of the protagonist and the drama. Sometimes, as the scene changes or the emotional intensity heightens, at the expressed wish of the protagonist, the action moves to another part of the room. Perhaps this echoes the levels of the Beacon stage.

Whether psychodrama happens in a specially designed room, a church hall, a hospital ward, a classroom or any other space and whatever the physical form of the stage, it has the same function. The stage or psychodrama working space is a place outside the 'real' world although rooted firmly in it. It is a place of safety in which the protagonist is free to experiment, a place where reality and fantasy work together. Anything may happen on the psycho-drama stage. It is 'an extension of life' (Moreno, 1953: 81), a place in which a person's reality can be constructed, their potential explored and a place to tell a story – 'this is how it is for me.'

The Essential Elements

Moreno (1953: 81–83) describes five 'instruments' as essential to the psychodramatic method. These are:

1 The stage (discussed above).
2 The protagonist, that is the person who is the subject of the psychodrama and its principal actor.
3 The director, who uses a set of professional skills to facilitate the enactment and to ensure the safety of the protagonist and the group.
4 The auxiliary egos (now most commonly called auxiliaries), who are the people who assist in the action by taking on roles.
5 The audience, who are the people witnessing the drama.

The Protagonist

In psychodrama, the protagonist is the person whose issue becomes the focus of the group's activity. Karp (1995: 295) writes, the protagonist 'is a representative voice of the group through which other group members can do their own work'. There may be more than one protagonist in the course of any psychodrama session but, usually, only one at a time. With the aid of the director and the collaboration of group members, protagonists explore scenes from their lives in which they play themselves and, when it is useful to the action, other people or things. These scenes may be of real incidents from the past or present of the protagonist or they may be imaginary, addressing what could have happened, what *should* have happened or things yet to be. A psychodrama may focus on the death of a parent, giving the protagonist the chance to say goodbye in a way that didn't happen. It may be that the issue is one of childhood trauma and that the protagonist takes the oppor-tunity to show the group how awful life was for the child she once was, giving testimony as the group bear witness. Another protago-nist may focus on the joy of friendship and the scenes be of communion, shared delights and a deep sense of companionship.

The possibilities are limited only by the experience and imagination of the group.

Whatever the course of the drama and whatever role the protagonists take, the focus is always on *their* experience. Although the director might invite the protagonist to reverse roles with another character in the drama, it is still the protagonist's perspective which remains the focus. How the protagonist perceives this other person to be is what matters and there is no attempt to investigate a situation from the perspective of another person, still less to establish some 'objective' reality. For example:

Judy was protagonist and chose to look at her unresolved anger. She recreated a scene in which she found her bicycle had been stolen due to the carelessness of a friend. Recognizing her bicycle in the street, she ran across to the rider and presumed thief and began to berate and assault him. As this scene was played out in the psychodrama session, Judy made it clear that she had unjustly accused this other person. The bike she had 'recognized' was not hers. Although at times the director asked Judy to play the presumed thief, no attempt was made to explore his feelings at being unjustly accused. This wasn't an issue for Judy, in fact she used this scene as a trigger to an exploration of other times in which she hadn't been able to find an appropriate outlet for her anger.

The Director

In psychodrama psychotherapy, the title director (or in, for example, the case of person-centred psychodrama, facilitator) is given to the principal therapist in a particular enactment. The director's function is that of a co-producer, putting a set of professional skills at the service of the protagonist in such a way as to facilitate the action. The director also has a responsibility to the auxiliaries and to the rest of the group. To a certain extent, directors must develop 'eyes in the backs of their heads' because, although it is important to focus on the protagonist, they must be constantly aware of what else is going on in the room, who is agitated or distressed, who has drifted off, and be prepared to do something about this if it seems necessary. This is perhaps slightly easier when two psychodramatists work together because the one who is chosen or elects to direct can rely upon their partner to take some responsibility for 'watching the group' but that still remains part of the director's task.

Psychodramatists from different traditions may have different understandings of how this is done and differ in the level of intervention they believe to be appropriate. For example, psychodramatists influenced by psychoanalysis attach less importance to their presence as a person than do those of an humanistic or existential bent and are more likely to offer an interpretation than to share their own experience. As a person-centred psychodramatist, I rely upon my empathic sensing of my protagonists as a way of understanding their perceptual worlds. This understanding informs the offers I make to them in the course of an enactment. In common with other person-centred practitioners, I believe that the relationship between therapist and client (or director and protagonist) is more important than theory and technique. A leading person-centred psychodramatist, Jenny Biancardi (personal communication, 1994) says that often the issue protagonists wish to explore is present in their relationship with the director from the outset of the psychodrama. The director can make use of this as a deliberate act. For example:

As facilitator, I had been working with Joe for about an hour. We had explored several very painful scenes from his childhood but it appeared now that we were stuck. I was out of ideas, I had a sense of 'losing' Joe. I couldn't tell what was happening for him and I just didn't know what to do. I felt very disappointed in myself. Then I heard Joe say again that a constant feature of his early life was of being disappointed and let down by his father. Whenever Joe needed him, his dad just seemed paralysed and unable to come up with anything useful. This time it clicked. I said to Joe, 'Whenever you were stuck, really needed some help, your dad was pretty useless. He just floundered around. He could see you were desperate but just couldn't do anything. And that is exactly what is going on here. You really need my help and I'm being bloody useless.' Joe just nodded and smiled in a relieved-looking way, but at this recognition it was as if a dam burst – somehow we were both enlivened and the action took off once more. It was as if Joe really needed an open acknowledgement of his experience of being continually let down before he could make progress.

Kellerman (1992: 45–57) discusses the professional roles of the psychodramatist. These are, as analyst with the task of empathizing and understanding, as producer with the function of theatre director and the responsibility to (p. 48) 'create a stimulating work of dramatic art', as therapist or agent of change towards growth and healing, and lastly, as group leader with the task of managing group process. Karp (1995: 294) lists twenty-three tasks of the psychodrama director. These include nine which precede the action, six which follow it, three which are to do with the boundaries or containment and only five which are concerned with the action itself. For me, this all bespeaks the complexity of the psychodrama director's role. In many ways, as pivotal to the whole process as it is, the action in a psychodrama group is but the tip of the iceberg. The director must do a great deal to establish the framework in which action can happen and psychodrama is as involving for the auxiliaries and the audience as it is for the protagonist. It is the director's job to be aware of and attend to this at all times.

The Auxiliaries

Moreno gave the name 'auxiliary ego' to those people other than the protagonist who took on roles in a psychodrama. Originally, auxiliary egos were co-therapists, drawn, for example, from staff and trainee therapists. Now, the term 'auxiliary' is preferred and it is most common for other members of the group to be chosen by protagonists to take on roles in their dramas.

Moreno (1985: 233) described the auxiliary ego as 'a therapeutic agent' who provides the assistance the protagonist needs in exploring or resolving a situation, issue or relationship. He believed that every person in a psychodrama group has the potential to be such a therapeutic agent to the others. Because of this, protagonists are usually invited by directors to pick the person in the group who seems the 'best fit' for the necessary role (which may be another person, an aspect of the protagonist or even an object). This choice is usually best made spontaneously and intuitively. The person picked need not be of the same sex, age or background as the person to be portrayed. As well as men, I have played women of all shapes, sizes and ages, a dead baby – even a wardrobe! Acting ability isn't necessary in the auxiliary, what is helpful is a willingness to respond spontaneously and creatively to a sense of role.

A core psychodramatic belief is that the protagonist will choose the most appropriate person for the role however unlikely that choice may seem at first. The process by which this happens, Moreno called *tele*, which is mutual appreciation and understanding. This may be a largely intuitive process. Often, it isn't until after the action that the 'reason' for the choice becomes clear. Feedback from auxiliaries often includes statements such as 'I knew you would choose me – my dad was just like that' or 'When I was younger, I was on the road just like the character I played.' For example:

At a large, international gathering, a protagonist had elected to work on his relationship with his father. Selecting auxiliaries from this very large group, he had established a scene in his childhood home. This was a family meal time. Father sat at the head of the table, the protagonist was amongst members of his extended family along one side. The protagonist's first language was different from that of the director and from the auxiliaries. When it became clear that the protagonist was struggling, the director said, 'How old are you in this scene?'

The protagonist replied, 'About seven.'

The director responded, 'I guess you wouldn't be speaking English then. Why don't you speak in your own language? The rest of us will manage.'

The protagonist immediately took the suggestion and addressed his 'father' in his first language. To the surprise of everyone, the auxiliary replied fluently in the same language. The psychodrama proceeded apace.

In sharing, the auxiliary who had played the father told the group that not only was he fluent in the protagonist's language (of which the protagonist had no previous knowledge) but that his partner was of the same nationality as the protagonist and from a comparable background. It transpired that the auxiliary had been present at many similar family meals.

The person chosen as auxiliary has the right to refuse but only rarely will the director intervene in the protagonist's choice, perhaps because of some knowledge of the potential auxiliary or a perception of the group need.

As well as being an important agent for change in protagonists, the experience of being an auxiliary may itself be therapeutic. Sometimes, there is an opportunity to take on a role which is aspired to; sometimes acting for the protagonist results in the auxiliary going some way to meet a personal need; sometimes it is a chance to experiment with or develop an aspect of the auxiliary's personality which is usually subdued or repressed. For example:

In the later stages of a psychodrama dealing with unresolved grief at the death of her young daughter, Carol asked Maria to play the part of her little girl, Nancy. Carol chose to meet Nancy in a quiet park where the two of them had gone so often to play. They sat on the grass and talked to each other, holding hands and hugging. Carol expressed the love she felt for Nancy and told her how much she was missed. Carol went on to declare how angry she was at being deprived of her beautiful daughter. Maria needed no direction – she responded instinctively in a way that was right for Carol. The group was enthralled as the pair demonstrated their love for each other.

*Eventually, Carol felt able to say goodbye to Nancy and, there in the park beloved by them both, there was a long and tearful farewell, sealed with a kiss. In **sharing** (the part of a psychodrama which follows the action itself) Maria told of her feelings as Nancy, and how that related to her own experience. She said that it had been extremely powerful for her. She connected with her own experience of being a mother and with her relationship with her own mother. Maria said that she felt deprived of maternal love and she had felt comforted, soothed and to some extent healed by the mothering she had received as Nancy. This was very important in Maria's development. She later went on to be protagonist in a drama which explored her relationship with her own mother. Sometime after this event, Maria said, 'You know how important and painful that psychodrama I did about my mum was? I don't think I ever would have had the courage if I hadn't been Nancy. Carol was such a good mum – I really got so much from her – it made me brave enough to face what a rotten mother my own was!'*

The Audience
In a psychodrama, the audience is all those people in the group not directly involved in the action. From the point of view of the protagonist, they serve the therapeutic function of witnesses. This alone can have a powerful effect – most of us recognize the benefit of being listened to, really *heard*. This is potentially additionally strong in psychodrama because the story is being told with more than words. Moreno (1953: 84) has written of the importance to the protagonist of the presence of an audience 'which is willing to accept and understand him'. Pitzele (1992: 6) points out the value to the protagonist of Moreno's invitation to the audience, 'Share your life.' This meant 'speak to the protagonist of your own experience about your problems'. That is not to say that the psychodrama audience has carte blanche to speak about anything and everything. In sharing, the invitation from the director to the audience is, 'Tell the protagonist of what in your own life you are reminded by the drama. What feelings do you share?'

Being in the psychodrama audience is not a passive function, it requires active involvement and it is a process from which may be gained 'both enjoyment and benefit' (Holmes, 1991: 8). The psychodrama audience serves not only the function of supporting the protagonist but is itself engaged in the therapeutic process. The protagonist's story may awaken issues for members of the audience and identification with the protagonist (or even one of the auxiliaries) may bring catharsis or insight. Casson (1997a: 43–54) has written at length about 'the therapeusis of the audience' and discusses the various ways in which witnessing action can benefit the watcher.

> *Derek was watching as Margaret enacted a scene about her sense of being stuck. Out of the tables, chairs and cushions in the room, she built a huge and tangled pile into the centre of which she inserted herself. In this position, Margaret spoke of how it was to be her, totally surrounded by an impenetrable tangle, unable to move, scarcely able to see further than the limits of the obstacle. Derek was fascinated. He watched and had an increasing sense of being somatically and emotionally involved. His whole body was alive with shakes and quivers and he was at once excited, sad, angry and confused. Feelings flittered past, intense but ever-changing. This was his story, his stuckness. He couldn't believe that it was shared nor that it could be given shape in that way.*

Margaret didn't get much further with her stuckness than to bring it into the psychodramatic space and so give it a physical presence. This wasn't important to Derek. For him, the power lay in this physical representation and the sense of no longer being alone. He now had words to describe how it was to be him. This he was sure was an opening of a doorway. He didn't know where it would lead and he was both scared and excited but at last there was some prospect of movement in his life.

The Stages of Psychodrama

A psychodrama takes on a certain shape – it comprises three phases, which are:

- warm-up
- enactment
- sharing

In different psychodramas and with different directors, these stages may take different forms, but they are always present. In a way, each of the terms is self-defining; thus warm-up is about preparing, getting ready, toning up as individuals and as a group; enactment is the phase in which the protagonist, through action, tells a story, experiments, addresses an issue; and sharing is a coming together of the group in such a way as to give expression to common experiences and emotions. Each stage has its own structure and its own therapeutic potential.

Warm-up

The warm-up serves to produce an atmosphere of creative possibility. This first phase weaves a basket of safety in which the individual can begin to trust the director, the group and the method. When the room has its arms around you it is possible to be that which you thought you couldn't, to express that which seemed impossible to express. (Karp, 1995: 296)

Marcia Karp puts it so well that it is almost unnecessary to say more about the aim of the psychodrama warm-up. Whatever its form or content, its purpose is to establish an atmosphere of trust, a place of safety. This is not the same as a risk-free environment. Therapeutic change often depends on taking risks. What is important is to establish a climate in which risk-taking is possible.

Holmes (1991: 8–9) identifies three 'significant functions' of the warm-up stage. These are:

1 To stimulate the creativity and spontaneity of group members.
2 To facilitate interactions within the group, increasing a sense of trust and belonging.
3 To help members focus on personal issues which they may wish to address through psychodrama.

As well as being a time of coming together, it is in the warm-up stage in which the protagonist is identified. In some forms of psychodrama, it is the director who selects the protagonist responding to a sense of *act hunger* or scarcely contained inner need (conscious or unconscious) to express or experience some emotion or behaviour through action. Of act hunger, Karp (1994: 57) writes 'the desire for most people in psychodrama is to complete an act that has not been completed in life'. Some directors prefer the protagonist to emerge from the group by consensus, election or self-declaration but in any case the consent and willingness of the group is necessary if the drama is to be a success. There are many techniques for warming up a group and selecting a protagonist. These are discussed in Chapter 5.

Enactment
The enactment stage of psychodrama is characterized by the protagonist and director working together to tell the protagonist's story through action. A psychodrama usually comprises a number of scenes, beginning and ending in the present and travelling through space and time between. There is no plan, 'no script, the drama is spontaneous, created in the moment by the protagonist, the auxiliary egos and the director' (Holmes, 1991: 9). In this way, a psychodramatic journey is from the outside of an issue towards its core, from what is easily accessible to what seems difficult or unknown. Group members and objects in the room are used to represent elements in these scenes. As in children's games, a chair can be anything – a boat, a television, an oak tree – the only limitation is human imagination. Psychodramatic scenes range from simple representations involving perhaps only two chairs, the protagonist and one other person to multi-role epics rivalling those of Cecil B. De Mille! For example:

Michael wanted to talk to his brother about the difficulties they were experiencing in their relationship. The director invited him to think of a place where this meeting could take place. It seemed to Michael that any real place known to one or other of them or both would complicate the issue, colour it in some way. He elected for a 'neutral' space and placed two chairs on the stage, angled towards each other. Although he could see that lots of other people were in some sense involved in his relationship with his brother (parents, siblings, partners), Michael insisted that he wanted only one auxiliary to take the other chair and to be his brother. The enactment was a dialogue between the brothers.

and:

John was recreating a place in which he was happy. This was a glade, deep in the heart of a deciduous wood, far from the beaten track. So detailed was his recall of this place that he used every member of the group to represent it. Some people took on the roles of the birds and mice, others were trees, even blades of grass where represented. The sharing John received concentrated on the feelings of peace and unity his auxiliaries had felt in his forest scene.

The enaction may focus entirely on 'real' scenes; that is, the events and places portrayed are as the protagonist remembers them. A typical psychodrama process is for the director and protagonist to work together to build a scene which is, in effect, a statement of the issue or problem in the present or recent past and to use this as a trigger for other scenes. Sometimes the director asks the protagonist if they are reminded of another time when they felt as they do in the scene, sometimes this trigger is spontaneous:

Andrea's first scene was in the dining room of the home she was leaving after twenty years. Before the action, she had told the director and the group that she wanted to do some work about her sense of sadness and loss at leaving this house in which her children had grown up.

Psychodramatically, Andrea was seated at what had been the family dining table wrapping her best dinner service in tissue. She was clearly full of sadness and, at the director's invitation, she spoke aloud her thoughts and feelings. Suddenly she stopped. Apparently out of the blue she said, 'I

*remember I was sitting at this table in this very same chair
when my sister came to tell me that my mum had dropped
dead in the supermarket. I couldn't believe it – I just felt so
stunned. She was a healthy woman, full of life and not at all
old. I'd only been married a few weeks. I was devastated.'*

*In response to his sense of her inner state, the director
asked Andrea if she would like to explore her feelings at the
loss of her mother. The action shifted through the years, the
auxiliaries changed and Andrea reconnected with the intensity of her feeling at that time.*

Action need not be confined to 'what happened' but can move
into **surplus reality**. This is the term given to the enactment of
events which never happened and never can happen, the voicing of
words never said.

*Following on from her re-capture of the events and feelings
on the day of her mother's death, Andrea expressed the desire
to talk to her mother, to tell her all the things that were left
unsaid. With the help of the director and the group, Andrea
established a scene in the house where she had been born and
where she and her mother had shared many times of great
warmth and closeness. Andrea spoke to her mother here,
telling her of the now grown-up grandchildren she never
knew, of how much she was missed and the sense of injustice
that Andrea carried to this day.*

Sharing

When the action draws to a close, the final phase of psychodrama
begins. This is a time for the auxiliaries to de-role, for the protagonist to reconnect with the group and for the other members to give
expression to their thoughts and feelings about what in their own
lives has been touched by the protagonist's story. Analysis and
advice-giving have no place in this sharing. Protagonists have taken
the risk of exposing themselves, allowing their hearts and souls to
be open to the group; they are likely to be in a very vulnerable and
delicate state. Criticism and interpretation are unlikely to be
helpful.

Sharing encourages identification with the protagonist in an
emotionally involved manner. In this way, the protagonist loses
some of the feelings of being laid bare and is enfolded once more
in 'the arms of the room'. Auxiliaries are encouraged to 'share from

role'. This is an opportunity to say how it felt to play the part. This may give the protagonist extra information but it is also a way of divesting powerful feelings which belong to the person being portrayed rather than the auxiliary.

Barbara is a social worker who was having some difficulty resolving tensions in her workplace. In Barbara's psychodrama, Helen had been playing one of her clients called Angela. In role, Helen had been sulky and silent, refusing Barbara's offers of help.

During sharing, Helen said, 'As Angela, I felt really powerful. Not talking to you was the one thing I could do without getting punished. And I could see it really wound you up. I liked that. I liked all the attention you were giving me too. I knew I'd always give you just enough back to keep that coming but there was no way I was going to do what you wanted.' Helen paused for a moment and then she said, 'But I'm not like that. I'm different from Angela because I don't keep people guessing – I tell them straight.'

Sharing is of therapeutic importance for the audience too. It is an opportunity to release powerful feelings stirred up by the action and for the agitated, vulnerable or emotional group member too to feel the arms of the group around them. Holmes (1991: 13) writes, 'the open sharing of these issues within the group encourages and facilitates support, caring and understanding between group members'. This is one of the many things that make psychodrama therapeutic for the whole group and not just the protagonist.

The Techniques of Psychodrama

In the enaction, directors have a number of techniques at their disposal. The ones they use to some extent depend upon their personal preference and theoretical understanding, but the overriding question directors ask of themselves is 'What would be helpful to the protagonist at this time?' In their chapter 'Principles of Psychodrama Techniques', Blatner with Blatner (1988: 151–157) describe a variety of basic and specific techniques and (p. 156) say 'the range of psychodrama techniques is potentially endless'. The most widely used psychodrama techniques include the following.

Role reversal

Role reversal is regarded by many psychodramatists as the most important, most fundamental, of their techniques. It is 'the engine that drives psychodrama'. It is the process by which the protagonist temporarily becomes someone or something else in their psychodrama by adopting the position, characteristics and behaviour of the 'other'. The auxiliary performing that role temporarily occupies the part of the protagonist.

Role reversal has many functions. In **scene-setting**, the part of a psychodrama where the context for the action (time, place, personnel) is established, it conveys to the group the protagonist's perception of important people in the drama and provides the auxiliaries with information from which to develop their roles. As the drama unfolds, it may be used to provide the group, auxiliaries and director with further information about the 'other'. For example, if an auxiliary is stuck or the protagonist senses that the person being played would not have responded as the auxiliary did, then the director will invite the protagonist to reverse roles: 'Show us how it would have been.'

Role reversal also enables the protagonist to see the world from the perspective of the other person. It is a strange fact but it often seems that the protagonist 'knows' more about the other when they become them, words are spoken, images come to mind, feelings are experienced of which, as themselves, the protagonist would seem to have no knowledge. Role reversal is a way of offering the protagonist deeper understanding of the process between themselves and other elements in their drama. Of this process, Kellerman (1992: 91) writes: 'Such a first-hand awareness may give the protagonist an experience which is sufficiently meaningful to produce a lasting impact.' For example (from Wilkins, 1995: 248–249):

> *Kate, a counsellor working in private practice, 'wanted to gain further insight into her relationship with Geraldine, a client with whom she felt stuck and of whom she was sometimes afraid'. In the course of the psychodrama, Kate reversed roles with Geraldine. In reverse roles, Kate's 'principal discovery was that Geraldine was intensely uncomfortable and frightened – and yet she desperately wanted to trust her counsellor. Kate experienced (herself as) Geraldine as very lonely, locked in a world from which she perceived no*

*escape – her disturbed (and disturbing) behaviour seemed to
result from attempts to break out from this internal prison.'
In sharing, Kate said 'that it was not until she "became"
Geraldine that she felt she had a true understanding of their
relationship'. Kate was able to use this new knowledge in her
work with Geraldine.*

Doubling

Doubling is now used as the name for two different techniques:
these are sometimes known as **permanent doubling** and **spontaneous doubling**.

PERMANENT DOUBLING   In traditional psychodrama, the double is a
member of the group who stands with the protagonist throughout
much or all of the drama, adopting their posture and mannerisms.
This kind of double has primarily a supportive function. Sometimes
the physical presence of an 'ally' is of itself helpful and enabling.
Through empathy, 'the double is able to express thoughts and
feelings that the protagonist is repressing or censoring in the
psychodrama' (Holmes, 1991: 11).

SPONTANEOUS DOUBLING   This form of doubling occurs when a
member of the group not otherwise in role has some sense of what
isn't being said or what might be helpful and – with the agreement
of both the director (who has the task of ensuring that the flow of
the action is not disrupted or deflected) and the protagonist –
offers this, speaking as the protagonist and while in contact with
them. As well as the insight it offers, an advantage to the protagonist of this form of doubling is that it gives a sense of the group's
involvement in and support for the drama.

In both kinds of doubling, protagonists may accept what doubles
say and repeat what has been said in their own words. Alternatively, if they don't fit, protagonists reject the words of the
double. Sometimes, the words of the double, although 'inaccurate',
stimulate the protagonist's self-awareness: 'No it isn't like that – it's
like this . . .'

Mirroring

Mirroring is a psychodramatic method for letting a protagonist
view a scene from the outside. The protagonist is replaced by an
auxiliary and leaves the scene and watches as the action continues
or is replayed. Blatner with Blatner (1988: 169) call this 'the human

version of videotape playback'. They also warn that mirroring is a powerful technique which 'must be used with discretion'. The purpose of mirroring is to encourage in the protagonist 'a more objective awareness of himself/herself in interactions with others'.

Finding a Psychodrama Psychotherapist and the Shape of Psychodrama

Anyone seeking psychodrama as therapy or for personal growth has a variety of choices. It is practised in a variety of settings and forms. It is primarily known as a group psychotherapy but is also offered one-to-one. Groups may meet regularly or may form for a 'one-off' session.

The Whereabouts of Psychodramatists

Psychodrama is available through health-care services (although access may be restricted to those with a perceived psychiatric need) and in some social service settings including some voluntary agencies, although again access is likely to be restricted to a particular client group. Outside of these agencies, psychodrama is most commonly available in the private sector. The services of psychodramatists practising privately are advertised and promoted in a variety of ways. Psychodrama training centres (see Chapter 8) sometimes offer open sessions and may very well be a source of information about the services of other psychodramatists.

Professional Standing of Psychodramatists

For their own protection, anyone seeking a psychodrama psychotherapist is well advised to choose from those who are members of reputable professional organizations. To be recognized as a practitioner by a professional organization, a psychodramatist must have undergone a recognized training and subscribe to a code of practice. In Britain, psychodramatists of standing are likely to belong to the British Psychodrama Association, in the USA to the American Society of Group Psychotherapy and Psychodrama, in Australasia there is the Australian and New Zealand Association of Psychodramatists, Sociodramatists and Role Trainers, and so on. What matters most is that the psychodramatist practises under the auspices of an association of good reputation, with a code of practice, a code of ethics and a procedure for complaints. Professional organizations may publish registers of their practitioner members or be able to help in other ways in putting would-be clients in touch with therapists.

Groups, Intensives and Psychodrama à deux

When psychodrama is offered as an on-going group, that is to the same people on a regular basis (most commonly weekly), such groups may be open-ended with members coming and going according to their individual contracts with the director and the group, or time-limited (lasting for a definite period, perhaps as little as ten weeks, perhaps for a year or more). Time-limited groups tend to be 'closed', that is comprising the same people for the whole of the duration. In this format, a typical psychodrama session lasts from one to four hours but most commonly about two-and-a-half hours. Experience in such a group is usually a prerequisite of psychodrama training.

In the form of a one-off intensive, psychodrama is offered as a workshop lasting a day, a weekend or even for a full week. Groups lasting more than one day are sometimes held in a residential setting, which adds to the intensity of the experience. It is even possible to find such psychodrama groups combined with a holiday in the sun on, for example, the Greek island of Skyros.

Psychodramatists are to some extent divided as to which of these formats is 'better'. Kellerman (1992: 21) presents both sides of the argument:

> Most practitioners agree that intensive workshops speed up the thera-peutic process because of the acceleration of self-disclosure, affective involvement and group cohesion. Once-a-week sessions proceed at a slower pace, but the continuity, gradual unfolding and repetitive work-ing through of central issues may help participants to integrate better gains made in psychodrama into their daily lives.

Psychodrama is less commonly offered one-to-one, with the therapist playing the roles of the director, auxiliaries, double and other functions as needed. This may be particularly appropriate with vulnerable or fragile clients or those for whom for any other reason a group setting is unsuitable or impossible. For example, Bannister (1991: 85) writes, 'young children are able to use psycho-dramatic techniques quite naturally, with the director acting as facilitator and supporter and as an auxiliary.'

Choosing a Psychodramatist

The choice of an appropriate form of psychodrama therapy is largely a matter for the would-be client. Issues of access ('Can I get away for a whole weekend?', 'Can I really give up twenty Thursday afternoons on the trot?', 'Just what psychodrama is there in my locality?') and cost are likely to play some part in the decision, but other things matter too. It is important that the potential client feels able to trust and work with the psychodramatist. In applying for an intensive group held in a distant part of the country to be led by someone unknown, there is an unavoidable element of risk. For an on-going group, it is possible, even usual to meet the psycho-dramatist(s) beforehand. This meeting may comprise a formal (but mutual) assessment or it may be a less formal opportunity to ask questions and for each person to gain preliminary insight into the other. Even for an intensive group for which there isn't an opportunity for a prior meeting, a telephone call should be possible.

If they aren't answered in the promotional literature or sponta-neously by the therapist, there are a number of questions a prospective psychodrama client might like to ask. These include:

- What is the professional standing of the psychodramatist?
- Will the psychodramatist be supervised for this work?
- What commitment is expected of me to the psychodramatist and the group?
- What will be the commitment of the psychodramatist to me?

My advice to any prospective recipient of psychodrama is to tune in to your own intuition, your spontaneity and creativity. What seems the most exciting, most promising form of psychodrama for you at this point? Follow your instinct, trust your process and you are likely to make a good decision.

3

WARMING-UP: LAYING THE FOUNDATIONS OF PRACTICE

The Importance of Training

The initial act of any psychodrama practice is the decision to embark upon a course of professional training. This may very well follow upon some experience of psychodrama in the client role, perhaps in a workshop, perhaps as a member of an on-going group. It is likely too that the would-be psychodramatist will have some experience in a helping role, for example, as therapist, nurse, psychiatrist, social worker, teacher or in a voluntary capacity. Karp (1995: 297) discusses psychodrama training and emphasizes its importance:

> Psychodrama training is a postgraduate training for mental health professions. It usually takes a minimum of two to three years after initial professional training. Psychodramatists have their own therapy and supervision as well as a primary trainer who follows their clinical and theoretical progress. Because psychodrama is a powerful therapeutic tool, only those trained in its use should be using it.

For somebody with an existing and developed knowledge of the theory and practice of psychotherapy and with sufficient resources (specifically of time and money), it may still be possible to train as a psychodramatist in two to three years, but four years is now a more realistic period.

Kane (1992: 43) also warns against the dangers of psychodrama practice from an inadequate base in knowledge and experience:

> Practitioners are inadequately trained if they do not go through rigorous procedures of establishing a theoretical base of knowledge regarding

group process and dynamics, psychology, personality, therapeutic processes, and drama. In addition to this knowledge base, a practitioner should have extensive experience, under training conditions, as an observer of, a participant in, a monitored and, finally, solo leader of classical psychodrama group sessions. . . . practitioners should never engage in special areas for which they are not trained and do not have credentials.

Although some of the techniques of psychodrama look simple and as if they would enrich any therapeutic practice, it would be unwise, probably unethical and perhaps dangerous to disregard the warnings of Karp and Kane. Good, professionally approved training is widely available (see Chapter 8). It is personally demanding of the trainee and takes time, effort and (often) money, but it can be richly rewarding and there really is no alternative for anyone wishing to practise as a psychodrama psychotherapist.

The exact nature of psychodrama training varies from accrediting organization to accrediting organization and, to a lesser extent (where these are different), from training organization to training organization. For example, in the United Kingdom psychodrama training is offered by a number of organizations approved by the British Psychodrama Association. Each institution offers a course based upon the interests and competence of its trainers – the Northern School of Psychodrama emphasizes a person-centred approach, the London Centre for Psychodrama and Group Analytic Psychotherapy adopts a psychodynamic framework and so on – but there are agreed broad similarities and each course leads to individual professional recognition by the United Kingdom Council for Psychotherapy.

In their training practitioners will have gained not only knowledge of the theory and practice of psychodrama and related disciplines but will have a sense of themselves in relation to clients and potential clients. In this context, Langley (1994: 12) refers to the importance of boundaries: these she lists as:

1 Knowing what you are doing and why. Having a theoretical base from which to work and to which you can refer for confirmation/validation of action.
2 Awareness of personal and professional limitations.
3 Boundaries to time, space and place.
4 Personal boundaries of physical contact.
5 Therapy/training/social boundaries. Personal and professional relationships.

6 Having respect for others, clients, colleagues and other professionals and their right to retain their own boundaries.

It is only when all this has become deeply ingrained but never-
theless regularly reflected upon and critically evaluated that the
practitioner is ready to meet with clients.

Preparing to Work with Clients
Successfully completing a course of training is the first step in a
psychodrama practitioner's warm-up. The second is preparing
psychologically and emotionally for client contact. It is a matter of
becoming ready to be a facilitator of a particular group in a
particular place at a particular time. This preparation precedes any
meeting with clients or potential clients. As well as orienting to the
physical space in which the group will meet and a consideration of
practical issues (see below), this will include a process of familiarization with the likely needs of a specific client group who might be
defined by (for example) their age, the setting in which they are to
be found (prison, hospital, school etc.), the way in which they
perceive themselves or are perceived by others (having an eating
disorder, seeking personal growth, hearing voices etc.) and so on.
This familiarization may involve reading, reflection, talking to
others who know something of the client group or any other
process which aids the practitioner to feel less anxious and
appropriately informed. In their preparation to act as co-therapists
for a group of women survivors of sexual abuse, Corti and Casson
(1990: 38) brainstormed the issues, thought about techniques and
exercises they might use and met with a specialist supervisor. They
also took time to meet informally 'to get to know each other more'
and 'discussed possible problems, our hopes and fears and also did
some reading'. Costa and Walsh (1991: 24–25) also emphasize the
importance of their pre-group preparations.

An important part of these preparations is supervision. As for
other branches of counselling and psychotherapy, there is an
ethical and professional obligation for psychodramatists to have
their clinical practice supervised. It is advisable that at least one
supervisory session takes place *before* the group meets and perhaps even before any initial meetings with potential clients. This
session would be an opportunity to air any fears and worries, for
practitioners to think about themselves in relation to the clients
and the working space and, in the case of two psychodramatists
working together, to address the dynamics of the ***co-therapy***

relationship. Anne Bannister (personal communication, 1995), an experienced psychodrama and dramatherapy supervisor, asks co-therapists to look at their own relationship and whether they have considered all the imbalances of power which might be present. She says too, 'We look together at gender, race, age, and (often importantly) hierarchical status, especially if they work for the same organization. We look at imbalances of experience, especially at working with a particular client group.'

The importance given to adequate psychological preparation of the director(s) cannot be over-emphasized. It does not matter that the client group, the setting, perhaps even the individuals are familiar; good preparation is the foundation of successful therapy and complacency is its enemy.

There are also a number of practical issues to be settled before pyschodramatists begin their work with any particular group of clients. Questions to answer include:

1   Who are the potential clients, how may they be informed about the group and what will attract them to it?
2   What are the conditions of group membership?
3   Where will the group meet? What is the nature of the space and what must I do to prepare it for psychodrama? Are there problems of access and, if so, how may they be overcome?
4   For how long will the group meet – both in terms of individual sessions and in terms of its total life?
5   On which day(s) and at what time will the group meet? Is this likely to cause problems with public transport, working patterns etc.?
6   What will the cost of this group be to its members? If they are to be charged a fee, how will this be collected?
7   What arrangements have been made for supervision and support and (if relevant) talking things over with my co-therapist?
8   What will be the nature of any pre-group meeting with potential group members? Is there to be a formal assessment process? Is there any paperwork which must be dealt with?
9   Do I have any responsibility to referrers and, if so, how can this be met?
10 What provision, if any, should be made for the support of group members between sessions?
11 How do I expect this group will end and what do I need to do *now* to ensure that ending?

12   How will I cope with the unexpected?
13   What have I forgotten?

The answers to these questions will vary between individual practitioners, the client group and the working setting. For example, I prefer to work as a co-therapist (because I and therefore my clients benefit from the collaborative relationship), to attract my clients by introducing myself and the aims of the group through some kind of promotional literature (such as posters, leaflets and the like) and to work in an informal but quiet and private space with which I am familiar or with which I previously familiarize myself. I am equally fond of working with groups who meet regularly (perhaps once a week for two or three hours) or intensively over a whole day or longer. I do not conduct a formal assessment but I do like to offer potential clients the chance to get to know me before committing themselves to working with me. Other psychodramatists prefer to work alone, some work in a purposely designed psychodrama space with a designated stage and for some referral and assessment are an important part of the process. For some practitioners, a group which is closed (that is, attended by the same people throughout its life, admitting no new members after an agreed initial period) and which meets regularly is seen as most effective; for others, it is the ability to work intensively over (for example) a day or a weekend, perhaps in a residential setting, which offers the greatest likelihood of change.

Many combinations are possible and each has its advantages and disadvantages. For example, when two psychodramatists work together as equals, they are co-therapists – this offers different opportunities from facilitating a group alone. Lone psychodramatists have responsibility for all that happens in their groups; in the co-therapy relationship these responsibilities are shared, although only one co-therapist at a time acts as director of a particular psychodrama. Some psychodramatists take the view that the presence of two therapists of equal status is confusing for the clients, that it can lead to division and dissension and (for some who take a psychodynamic view) complicate the transference relationship. An opposing view is that the presence of co-therapists offers the clients greater choice (with my co-therapists, I encourage protagonists to choose the director they prefer and, usually the other of us is available as an auxiliary), perhaps contributes to feelings of security (for both clients and the co-therapists) and that it enhances the transference relationship, especially if the co-therapy pair is of mixed sex. There is little evidence to support either of these positions but an unpublished survey of British psychodramatists demonstrates a widely held view that established mixed gender co-therapists who are clear with each other and the group about the nature of their working relationship offer (for example) variety, choice, increased safety and the possibility of a heightened expression of varying male and female perspectives. It is important to emphasize that, regardless of whether they favoured it as a way of working or not, almost all of the seventy respondents to this survey stressed the importance of clarity, openness and good supervision in the co-therapy relationship. As with so many things in psychodrama (and other approaches to psychotherapy), it seems that, as long as the potential clients are able to make an informed choice, what works best is what the practitioners are most comfortable with and believe in.

Meeting the Clients

A psychodramatist who is adequately trained, is psychologically prepared, has decided upon the nature of the group, is familiar with the working space and has answers to a host of practical issues is at last in a position to recruit, meet with and select potential clients. How this is done again varies between practitioners and with client groups. Some psychodramatists favour a formal process of referral and assessment, others take an informal approach. This may reflect the philosophy of the practitioner. For example, formal assessment may be seen as an essential part of psychodynamic practice but many person-centred practitioners would see it as imposing something from the perspective of the therapist and therefore to be avoided. It may be about the work setting and accountability. Psychodramatists working in or for any bureaucracy (for example, a health care institution) and/or with clients who are labelled 'ill' or 'difficult' are likely to adopt different procedures from those working in private practice and whose clients self-refer for 'personal growth'. Holmes (1995: 96) distinguishes between two initial procedures in his own practice. When he recruits people for psychodrama workshops (which are not aimed at a 'patient' population) he does not formally assess but treats 'all group members as my equal and [expects] them to act in an appropriate manner and to take responsibility for their own actions'. However, he believes that for his on-going treatment groups 'more formal' assessment is necessary 'for the sake of the individual and of the group'.

Although there are differences in recruitment, selection and 'assessment' procedures between psychodramatists these may be more superficial than they at first appear. Gill (personal communication, 1998), in his investigation of the assessment procedures used by psychodynamic therapists and person-centred therapists working in medical settings, reports that, although the language used about initial contact between therapist and client varies between the two groups, what actually happens is broadly similar. Tantum (1995: 9) lists some goals of 'the first therapeutic interview'. These are:

1 Establishing a rapport with the patient.
2 Obtaining pertinent information:
    (a) Making a clinical diagnosis
    (b) Assessing the strengths and weaknesses of the patient
    (c) Determining aetiology
    (d) Evaluating the dynamics (eg. inner conflicts, mechanisms of defence).
3 Giving information.
4 Enabling the patient to feel understood, and giving hope.
5 Providing a therapeutic account.
6 Giving the patient a taste of the treatment.
7 Motivating the patient to pursue treatment.
8 Arranging for further assessments.
9 Selecting patients for treatment.
10 Selecting treatments for the patient.
11 Making practical arrangements for therapy.

Although these goals are stated in the language of the medical and psychoanalytic models, a person-centred practitioner would have serious reservations only about point 2 but would approach points 7, 8, 9 and 10 with caution.

Whatever the nature of assessment procedures, the intention of the ethical practitioner is to ensure a 'good fit' between therapist(s) and client. It is a mutual process and is about giving clients enough information to make an informed consent as to whether this way of working, this group, this psychodramatist is right for them at this time. Tantum (1995: 16) provides a useful list of the information clients might want from the therapist in order to make *their* assessment:

1 How does the treatment work?
2 How does it compare with other treatments?
3 How much does it cost?
4 How long does it take?
5 What are the qualifications of the therapist?

45

6   Is the patient discussed with anyone else?

7   Is what the patient says confidential?

The initial meeting is also an opportunity for the psychodramatists to make a decision about their ability to work with the potential client in the particular setting. Issues for psychodramatists to consider include the level of their knowledge and experience and the safety and welfare of the group as a whole. This is not always an easy process.

Bill and Jean had agreed to act as co-therapists for a psychodrama group and had been through the appropriate preparatory stages. They had advertised their group on noticeboards in community centres, public libraries, local colleges and through leaflets distributed to friends and colleagues. These posters and leaflets briefly explained the psychodrama process, gave some details of the background, training and experience of Bill and Jean and made it clear that the group was open to people who thought they would benefit from it. There was also information about the place and time of meeting, the duration of the group and its cost and an address and telephone number with an invitation to contact the co-therapists to find out more or to ask questions.

Bill and Jean dealt with the telephone enquiries in what they hoped was a warm, open and friendly manner and invited potential members to meet with them before committing themselves to joining the group. Anyone expressing an interest in this was individually invited to meet with Bill and Jean in the room in which the group would meet. These meetings were for about twenty minutes and held in the two weeks before the group was due to start. Bill and Jean did not see this as 'assessment' but as an opportunity for the potential group members to 'check out' the venue and the therapists and to have the chance to ask further questions. In principle, they saw this as a process by which the potential client could make an informed choice about joining the group. As they believed that clients are capable of making the decision as to whether a way of working is right for them, the issue of rejecting people did not arise. This was their usual way of introducing themselves to clients and, normally, it seemed to work.

On the second day of these informal meetings, Bill and Jean were waiting for Kirsty; their last potential client. She was late and they were beginning to think about giving up on her when the door burst open and, with little ceremony, a small, thin and pretty woman flung herself into the vacant chair and began to tell a tale of various horrors in her life. Jean tried to interrupt to introduce herself and Bill and to acknowledge Kirsty but the torrent of words continued. The tale was of Kirsty's sexual harassment by others, her own sexual predation, of torture, isolation and desperation. Somehow, it was less the content of what Kirsty said and more the way in which she said it that was disturbing and disorienting. Although both experienced therapists, Bill and Jean were in some sense overcome by Kirsty, not knowing how to respond to her. Kirsty left as abruptly as she had arrived saying that she was sure that psychodrama was right for her and that she would be at the first session the next week.

After Kirsty left, Bill and Jean just stared at each other for a while, uncertain as to what had happened or what to say about it. Eventually Jean broke the silence airing her grave doubts about Kirsty's suitability as a group member. Bill agreed about Kirsty's likely effect upon the group (and the co-therapists) but countered with an argument about what seemed to be her obvious need and the client's right to choose. Although it was rapidly clear that Bill and Jean agreed that they would not, indeed ethically could not, take Kirsty into the group, the discussion went on for some time. What they were looking for was a rationale for the action they instinctively knew to be right and a way of communicating to Kirsty their decision in a such a way as to indicate an understanding of her need and so mitigating the effects of rejecting her as a group member. They involved their supervisor in their deliberations, eventually resolved their dilemma and came up with a practical solution to the immediate problem of Kirsty. They decided to phone Kirsty and to explain that they thought that at this time the kind of psychodrama they could offer was not what she required. They also would make her the offer of seeing Jean for individual work or referring her to another psychotherapist.

Bill and Jean take an informal approach to assessment – indeed, they would not call the process by which they meet with and

introduce themselves to clients assessment at all. In their view it is
about enabling the potential group member to make a choice. Only
exceptionally do they make a decision as to the suitability of the
client. For others, assessment is a much more structured activity.

*Alison is a psychodramatist working in a psychiatric set-
ting. Based on her own experience and what she knew from
others, she decided that psychodrama would be an effective
way of working with people who have an eating disorder.
After talking over her ideas with her clinical supervisor and
her line manager, she was able to create time in her working
week in which she could offer psychodrama to this client
group. Alison then set about informing her colleagues and
other professionals (psychiatrists, community psychiatric
nurses, general practitioners, specialist services and so on)
of this opportunity, explaining to them what might happen
in a psychodrama group and why it was an effective way of
working with people with an eating disorder. This she did by
talking to people she knew and by circulating an explanatory
leaflet in which she referred to the evidence in the literature
making it clear that she sought appropriate referrals.*

*When she received a referral, Alison acknowledged it in
writing, informing referrers that she would keep them
appraised of the client's progress but emphasizing the confidential nature of a psychodrama group. In Alison's view
this is a necessary professional courtesy. Alison also con-
tacted the potential client explaining who she was, what
service she was offering and proposing that they meet to
discuss how and if being a member of the group would be
beneficial.*

*In these initial meetings (for which a whole hour was
allowed), as well as explaining about psychodrama and
checking that the potential client saw it as relevant to their
needs, Alison conducted a formal assessment, of which she
made a written record. This included biographical detail, a
contact address and telephone number, a note of any other
professional or service with whom the client was involved
and the name and address of the general practitioner with
whom the client was registered. Alison also asked about the
nature of the eating disorder and how it affected the client's
life. She then worked with the client to establish what reason-
able goals might be achievable through psychodrama. If*

Alison and the client thought that these goals were realistic and that the group was an appropriate vehicle for change at this time, the final stage in this process was to agree a contract in which Alison's responsibilities to the client and the client's responsibilities to Alison and other members of the group were made clear. If Alison had doubts about the suitability of the proposed group for the potential client then she said so, stating her reasons clearly and carefully. She also discussed what other options there were. For Alison, the process was completed by letting the referrer know the outcome of this meeting.

Whatever the nature of the assessment or introductory process, it is only when it is completed and some kind of contract agreed between the prospective participants and the psychodramatist(s) that a psychodrama group is ready to meet.

4

SCENE-SETTING:
GETTING STARTED

There are probably as many ways of introducing a new group to the techniques of psychodrama and establishing a sense of group identity as there are psychodramatists. What follows is an illustration of some of the issues to be addressed and examples of what might happen in the first two or three sessions with a group of people new to psychodrama. In some groups this will happen more quickly, in others more slowly. The client group, the preferred style of the psychodramatist and the number and length of the sessions will all influence what is done, how it is done and how long it takes.

The First Group Meeting

When a psychodrama group first meets it is likely that at least some and possibly all of its members will be new not only to each other and to the group leader but also to psychodrama. The immediate task of the psychodramatist is to facilitate some sense of group identity and to enable the establishment of a trusting atmosphere in which change, growth and healing may occur. In this, the beginning stages of a psychodrama group are like the beginnings of any other group meeting for psychotherapy or personal growth. It is a time of getting acquainted, determining how the group will function and a time for each member to find a place and a way of being in it. Group members (and perhaps the therapist) will be to a greater or lesser extent anxious, uncertain of what will happen and, because of this, tentative as they attempt to discover and test boundaries and wonder whether they will be accepted. It is the psychodramatist's job to ensure that group members begin to encounter each other (perhaps through something as simple as one of the variety of 'name games') and that they have an early opportunity to air their fears and expectations and to establish the formal group rules and norms.

Alongside this is the need to introduce the techniques and processes of the psychodramatic method. As Holmes (1995: 90–91) points out, action methods are rarely if ever used as part of the 'assessment' process for psychodrama and, however well these have been described in any promotional literature or face-to-face meeting, it is not until they are experienced that they are understood. Understanding of the techniques is a necessary precursor to psychodrama proper and a gentle, systematic introduction to them is the best way of helping to overcome any anxiety and disbelief group members may have. Fortunately, establishing a group climate and introducing psychodrama are processes which can go hand in hand because the latter offers much to induce the former.

When names have been spoken and perhaps each group member has had the opportunity to make some short statement about themselves, it is often most useful for the group (with the therapist) to decide upon the framework of rules within which it will operate. Some of these will be predetermined (for example, time and place of meeting, duration of sessions) but others must be agreed. These may include some decisions about late arrival and absence and, most importantly, a definition of confidentiality.

Knowing explicitly what 'confidentiality' means in the context of any particular group is essential to the establishment and maintenance of trust. Although an appreciation of the importance of confidentiality is widely held by group therapists of all kinds, there is sometimes an assumption that an understanding of the term is universally shared. This is not necessarily true. Additionally, group members often have unrealistic expectations of themselves and others with respect to confidentiality. Psychodrama is exciting, challenging, awakens feelings, brings to mind unfinished business, raises doubts and uncertainties not only for protagonists but for auxiliaries and audience too – it is a group approach involving everybody present. These powerful feelings usually need processing in some way and there may not be enough time or opportunity in the group. Also, they may relate to other people in an individual group member's life – and this may have to be dealt with outside the group.

What happens in a psychodrama group *will* be talked about outside the group. Finding a safe and respectful way of doing this to which all the group members can agree is important. The interweaving of personal stories characteristic of psychodrama makes it very difficult for group members to talk about only their own experience. How can group members tell a partner about their experience as auxiliary (which may have crucial bearing on their own development) without some reference to the protagonist? If it is allowable to make reference to others, how can this be done in a way which protects them and preserves their anonymity? People are identified by their names but also their roles, where they work or live, their ages, their character etc. If group members cannot speak freely about the group during its lifetime, can they do so at a specified time in the future? There are many other questions and each group will have its own solutions to the problems they raise. As a group leader, I like to make sure that the group is aware of the issues and to stress the importance of respecting each other, what we say and how we say it. I also point out that whatever contract we establish may, if necessary, be revisited and renegotiated.

Trust
Corey (1994: 96–97) discusses the importance of trust in group-work. He points out that the consensus amongst writers is that trust is essential to the continued development of a psychotherapy group. He states: 'Without trust, group interaction will be super-ficial, little self-exploration will take place, constructive challeng-ing of one another will not occur, and the group will operate under the handicap of hidden feelings.' A successful psychodrama group depends upon the group members trusting the psychodramatist, each other and the psychodramatic method. None of these arises as a matter of course. The agreed group rules provide a framework but it is not until these are experienced as upheld and seen to work that they can contribute to an atmosphere of trust. Trust has to be learned and earned. What most facilitates and promotes trust is the group leader's ability to show that the group can be a safe place in which to be real, open and honest. For me, this is about being empathic (that is sensitive to the inner experience of others), congruent (real, present without artifice and with my outer self being an accurate reflection of my inner self) and most importantly accepting. If I am real, responding in a genuine manner, if I sincerely attempt to understand how another person is feeling and communicate that understanding while accepting them for who

they are, where they are and how they are, and I do this con-
sistently, then the likelihood is that, over time, I will be trusted.
Other psychodramatists may express this differently but the basic
aims and strategies will be similar. In the context of psychodrama,
earning trust is also about introducing its techniques at a pace
appropriate to the particular group and in such a way as to allow
group members to express their doubts and reservations. Coombes
(1991: 19–47) writes about trusting the method in psychodrama
and discusses how to promote this trust and what might interfere
with its establishment.

Corey (1994: 96) expresses the opinion that encouraging group
members to talk about factors which inhibit their trust is conducive to establishing a therapeutic atmosphere. In psychodrama,
as in other group approaches, this is an early task. It is also useful
to facilitate the expression of doubts, fears and expectations and
to allow group members the opportunity to express how they feel
about being in the group. Depending upon their theoretical orientation and the nature of the group psychodramatists may or may not
participate themselves in introductory exercises. The following
example is drawn from my own practice; others would do it
differently.

It was the first meeting of the psychodrama group. The eight
members and the leader, Paul, had already learned each
other's names and agreed a group contract. Paul moved to the
centre of the room dragging a chair with him. 'This chair', he
said, 'represents the group or perhaps for you it is psycho-
drama in general. What I would like you to do is to find a
place in the room which somehow reflects how you feel about
whatever this chair represents to you now. I suggest you just
walk around the room until you find the place that feels most
comfortable to you. Don't think about this too much, just
follow your instinct, your intuition. This might be about
where other people put themselves as well as the chair, the
group, psychodrama or whatever it is. When you have found
somewhere, just stand still and I will come round, make
contact with you and then I would like you to say something
about why you have chosen that position and perhaps some-
thing about how you feel.'

All nine milled around for a while until, one by one, they
came to a halt. Paul was towards the edge of the room, a few
paces from the centre of a wall. He said, 'OK – is everybody

53

where it feels best to be?' There was a mixture of affirmative replies. 'Right,' said Paul. 'Now you have the chance to say something about why you are where you are. I'll go first – that seems only fair.

'For me, the chair is this group, us as we come together for the first time. I am a little way away from it at the moment but I am facing it and can see it clearly – that is important to me. I can see all of you too and I like that. Standing here I feel ready to move. Ready to move towards the group and into action.'

Paul then left his position and made his way to where Donna was standing. He placed his hand upon her shoulder and she said, 'I am here because I really wanted to be by the window. I don't know why, it just seemed right. I can see the group and that's nice – but I don't want to be any closer at the moment.'

Paul walked on to Gwen, who was lying on the floor about half-way between the chair and the wall. As Paul bent and touched her shoulder, she said, 'I'm feeling really laid back and easy. I just want to flop around on the floor. I tried standing up but it wasn't right. I like being here. I can't see many of you but I know you're there.'

Next came Fred. He was standing almost in the middle of the room with one foot touching a chair leg. He said, 'I'm here because I feel that I really want to reach out and touch the group. I'm already beginning to feel that I know you and I really want to get on with some psychodrama.'

Betty was in the doorway. 'I'm really not sure I want to be part of this group at all. It is all I can do to prevent myself from rushing out the door and going home.'

Roy was also near the door. He said, 'I'm here because I like to feel that I can get out if I want to – but actually I feel OK. I quite like it here. I can see everybody and I am quite close to Betty and to Paul. I like that.'

Sue was still in the chair she had occupied earlier in the session. She said, 'I just didn't want to move. I don't seem to have any energy. I thought about going a bit nearer to the group but I'm all right here.'

Dorothy had placed herself in the far corner of the room and she had her back against the wall. 'I came here to get away from everybody,' she said. 'I can't stand the thought of

*being close at the moment. It's nothing to do with the group –
it's just me – that's how I am.'*

Lastly, Paul came to Bernie, who was sitting on a chair he
had moved to about two metres from the group chair and
facing it. As Paul touched his shoulder, talking to the chair,
Bernie said, 'I put myself here because I really want to get to
know you. It was important to be on your level which is why
I got my chair and although I want to be close, I'm not yet –
so I wanted to stay at a bit of a distance. I'm feeling curious,
excited and a bit scared.'

Everyone in the group had spoken. Paul went back to his
own place and asked if anyone had anything else to say and
did anyone want to change their position. Dorothy took two
paces away from her corner and smiled shyly. 'Anyone else?'
said Paul, 'No? OK, let's get back into a circle and we'll carry
on.'

After taking some time to talk about how it had been to
place themselves in relation to the chair, the group decided
that they were ready for something else. Reaching into the
tattered supermarket carrier bag he had brought with him to
the session, Paul pulled out a crumpled felt hat and placed it
on the floor.

'I call this "Fear in the Hat," ' he said, as he tore a piece of
paper into nine strips. 'What I would like you to do is to take
a piece of paper and to write on it something you are
frightened of, apprehensive about, makes you wary – whatever. Some fear or worry you have about being in the group.
Don't sign it or indicate who you are on it – the idea is that
this is anonymous.

'When you have done that, fold it up and put it in the hat.
When we have all done that I'll come round and we will each
take one out and then take turns to read it to the rest of the
group. If you get your own don't worry – the rest of us won't
know.'

Everybody took a piece of paper and took it back to their
seat. Some wrote instantly, some looked thoughtful or hesi-
tant, but after two or three minutes there were nine pieces of
folded paper in the hat.

'OK,' said Paul picking up the hat, 'I'll come round now
and each of us will take out a piece of paper. You can read the
one you take out but wait until everybody has got one and
had a chance to look at it before we read them aloud.' Paul

took the hat round the group, taking the last piece of paper himself. One by one, what was on the pieces of paper was read out:

'I am frightened that I will get upset or emotional in this group.'

'I am worried that I will let people down by not being able to engage as much as I want.'

'I might lose control of my emotions.'

'I'm worried that people won't like or accept me.'

'I'm scared that if I let you see me, you won't like me.'

'I'm scared because I don't know what is going to happen.'

'I don't know whether I am going to be able to do this – and if I can't it means I'll let the rest of you down and that's scary too.'

'I'm scared that you won't accept me.'

'I'm frightened of exposing myself and being rejected.'

After all the fears had been read aloud, the group was quiet and thoughtful.

'All right,' said Paul. 'I wonder what it was like to hear your own fear read by somebody else and to hear everybody else's? And what was it like to read the one you got?'

Donna looked again at the piece of paper in her hand. 'What really struck me,' she said, 'was that I could have written this – I didn't, but I could have done. I could have written any of them.'

'Yeah,' said Bernie, 'that's right. There was something really comforting in hearing that all my fears were shared by the rest of you.'

'I am not so scared now,' said Betty. 'It was really strange hearing my fear read out. It is still real for me but hearing it read by somebody else makes it easier to live with somehow. And I agree with Donna and Bernie too – knowing that I am not the only one scared of all those things makes a huge difference. I really did think it was just me.'

Other group members expressed similar thoughts. It seemed that everybody was surprised that their fears were shared, and was comforted by this. Somehow hearing their own fears voiced made them less threatening.

The story above revolves around only two of many possible introductory exercises and they are not unique to psychodrama.

However, as well as being about building group trust and group cohesion, they do serve as an introduction to some basic ideas from psychodrama and sociometry. The group sculpt introduces the idea that spatial relationships play some part in the expression of thoughts and feelings – this is an important part of psychodramatic enaction. In it an inanimate object (the chair) takes on a role – that things can represent people and people represent things is basic to psychodrama. The sculpt itself is a 'snapshot' of relationships within the group and thus a sociometric exercise. 'Fear in the Hat' introduces the idea of speaking with the voice of another and so relates to being an auxiliary and *doubling*. Also the shape of a psychodrama session has been introduced. There has been a warm-up (getting to know names and setting a contract), enaction (the group sculpt and 'Fear in a Hat') and sharing (the opportunity to say what it was like to voice the fear of another and to connect with the fears heard).

The Second Group Meeting

Once a new group has had a chance to get to know a little bit about each other and the group leader and have aired their fears, hopes and expectations most psychodramatists begin to explicitly introduce the techniques of their modality. Members of a psychodrama group have to become familiar with the ideas of (for example) taking roles, setting scenes, role reversal and doubling. It is possible to explain what each of these is but most psychodramatists as well as offering some kind of explanation will take note of the invitation of the psychodrama director to the protagonist 'Don't tell us, show us' and will introduce the various aspects of psychodrama by inviting the group to participate in them.

Fundamental to psychodramatic action is the establishment of a scene, that is, the creation of a place and time, real or imagined, from past, present or future within the confines of the group space. A basic scene-setting exercise can introduce many elements of psychodrama and continue the process of building group cohesion. For example:

> *It was the second session of the psychodrama group facilitated by Jo and Pete. When they and the group members had each said a few words about how they were feeling that evening and what had happened since the last session, they explained that the group would do some scene-setting.*

Jo said, 'We'd like all of you to think about a place where you feel safe and comfortable. Perhaps it is somewhere you know, perhaps you go there a lot, perhaps it isn't real but somewhere you would like to be able to go. It doesn't really matter – what is important is that it is a special place to you and that you feel good about being there. What we invite you to do is take some time to think about this place. Then there will be an opportunity to talk to someone else in the group about your special place. Finally, one or perhaps two of you will have the chance to show us your place using the people and things here to do that. I know that is hard to imagine and don't worry about it just now. If you want to do it, one of us will help you – that's our job!'

Pete got to his feet and walked to the centre of the room. 'OK,' he said, 'find a place where you can feel relaxed, at ease and start to think about a place where you feel safe and comfortable. If it helps, you might like to follow my suggestions. If it doesn't, just ignore me and do your own thing.'

Some of the group members moved to other chairs or other parts of the room, some stayed where they were.

'Close your eyes,' said Pete, in his deep, soft voice, and, pausing between each suggestion. 'In your mind's eye begin to recall this special place. A place where you feel safe and comfortable. What can you see? What shapes and colours? What can you hear? What can you taste and smell? Is there anyone or anything else with you? How does it feel to be in your special place? Take your time, allow yourself to really be there.'

After a few minutes, Jo said, 'OK. Now find a partner, someone to share something about this place with. In your pairs, each of you will have the opportunity to say as much or as little about your special place as you wish. You'll have twelve minutes and we suggest you take it in turns – one of you listens while the other speaks. We will tell you when you are half-way through.'

The group members quickly sorted themselves into pairs and settled down to the task. Jo went over to where Pete was sitting and sat beside him. Some pairs were laughing, some looked intensely engaged with each other, but all seemed engrossed.

'You've had six minutes,' said Pete. 'If you haven't changed round, perhaps you could do so now.'

*And later, 'Just a minute left now. Do you need more
time?'*

*All the pairs finished the exercise within the twelve min-
utes and, at the invitation of Jo and Pete, pulled their chairs
into a circle and took the opportunity to share something
about how it had been to recall a special place and to hear
about the place of another.*

*'Would anybody like to make their special place here in this
room? To share it with us?' asked Pete. There were a few
minutes of silence.*

*'I wouldn't mind if nobody else wants to,' said Sandra, 'but
I don't know how I could.'*

*'That's OK,' said Pete. 'We know some ways of helping but
let's just check if anybody else wants a go. Anybody? No? Well
I guess, if you still want to Sandra, the floor is yours. Who
would you like to work with you, me or Jo?'*

'Jo, I think,' said Sandra. 'Is that all right?'

*'Yes,' said Jo, rising from her seat and going to sit next to
Sandra. 'I'm happy to work with you.*

*'So – what can you tell us about this place? Where is it?
Does it have a name?'*

*Sandra said, 'It's a beach back on the island where I was
born. I used to go there a lot with my mum. We'd have picnics
and go swimming. It was always warm and sunny and I
miss the sun!'*

*'OK,' said Jo. 'It's a beach back home. Shall we have a go at
bringing it here?'*

'How?' said Sandra.

*'Well, I guess we'll find out as we go along. Can we start by
finding a place in the room to be the beach? Does it have a
name?'*

*'Yes, we used to call it Pink Bay because of all the pink
flowers – and the rocks were a sort of pink too.'*

*'Right. Whereabouts in the room would you like to make
Pink Bay?' asked Jo.*

*'I think over there by the window – at least it looks a bit
sunny,' said Sandra.*

*'Let's go over there then,' said Jo, and she followed Sandra
across the room.*

*'All right, Sandra. We're standing in Pink Bay are we?' she
asked.*

59

'*Yes, we're on the path coming down from the village just at the point where you can first see the sand and the sea. It's all shady and woody up to here and then all of a sudden there is all this pink and gold and blue and it's so bright it almost makes your eyes hurt.*'

'*So, we are on the path and we can see the beach?*' asked Jo. '*Let's see if we can use the people and the things to make it a bit more real – I don't know if that is the right word – to bring it here somehow. Tell me what you can see.*'

'*I can see the sand – it stretches for miles and the sea, the waves. There is an old raft out there – we used to swim out to it and dive off.*'

As Jo stood at Sandra's side it was as if she too could see Pink Bay, awash with sunlight. '*An old raft,*' she said, '*is that important? Would you like it in your scene?*'

'*Yes, I think I would.*'

'*OK, what or who could be the old raft? Don't think about it too much. It often seems that it works best if you just go with the first thing that occurs,*' Jo said.

'*I think Bob – is that all right Bob?*' asked Sandra. Bob nodded.

'*So Bob can be the old raft,*' said Jo. '*Whereabouts is the raft – can you show us? Perhaps you could go and be the raft for a minute. This will give the rest of us some idea about what it was like and I guess that will be particularly helpful to Bob.*'

Sandra walked to the middle of the room and laid down on her belly, arms and legs outstretched.

'*You're an old raft floating in Pink Bay,*' said Jo. '*I wonder what you can tell us about yourself?*'

'*It's old and . . .*'

'*Could you speak as the old raft,*' interrupted Jo. '*That's what you are at the moment.*'

'*Oh,*' said Sandra, '*all right. I'm old – I have been here ages. Children swim out to me and climb on to my back – then they jump off laughing and screaming.*'

'*What can you see, old raft?*' asked Jo.

'*Not much, just the deep water. But I hear a lot. The children, their parents calling from the beach, the seagulls.*'

'*Is there anything more we should know about you, old raft?*' asked Jo.

'Even though I look old and rickety, I'm very safe,' said Sandra firmly.

'Right – could you come back to being Sandra now and we'll let Bob become the old raft. Is there anything else you need to know about yourself as the old raft Bob? No? Well please come and be the old raft floating in the sea at Pink Bay – just take up the place and position that Sandra showed us.'

'What else is there here?' said Jo to Sandra, as they stood together once more on the path leading to the beach.

'Oh – there is an enormous tree over there. How could I have forgotten? We used to spend hours climbing that when it was too hot to sit in the sun and we were tired of swimming. It was tall and shady and strong.'

'It *is* tall and shady and strong,' said Jo. 'OK – do you need the tree in your scene?'

'Yes I do – but it is so big and tall it is going to be a problem. Can I have more than one person?' asked Sandra.

'It's your scene – you can have whatever you like.'

Sandra looked round at the rest of the group. 'I'd like Liam, Sarah and Jamie to be the tree because you're all so tall.'

'Can you show them how you want them to be?' asked Jo. 'It's a bit more difficult when there is more than one but perhaps if you took them one at a time and told them something about themselves as the tree?'

Sandra took the three she had chosen and showed them how to stand, arms stretched up in the air and twined round each other. When she had finished she came and stood by Jo again.

'Is that right?' said Jo.

'No,' said Sandra, 'they're not tall enough – I want them to be higher.'

'How can you do that?'

'Could they stand on the chairs? Will that be all right?'

'Give it a try,' said Jo.

Liam, Sarah and Jamie all stood on chairs. Jo asked Sandra to take the place of each one of them in turn and to say something as the tree.

'What three words would you use to describe yourself, tree?'

'Strong, wise and protecting,' was Sandra's reply from each position.

And so Sandra went on building Pink Bay. Members of the group became seagulls, turtles basking in the sun, waves and the pink flowers which gave the place its name. When she had finished, Jo invited her to stand and look and to feel again what it was like to be at Pink Bay. As Sandra stood and watched her scene it seemed as if many different emotions crossed her face.

'Is there anything you would like to say to Pink Bay, to your special place, before we leave it?' asked Jo.

'Yes,' sighed Sandra. 'I miss you so much – I was so happy here. I wish I could stay.' Tears filled her eyes.

'I guess there are some sad things about even the loveliest, safest places,' said Jo, 'especially when we are parted from them.'

Sandra nodded.

'Is there anything else you need to do before we leave the scene?' asked Jo.

'I don't think so,' said Sandra.

'OK,' said Jo, 'then it is time to take the scene apart – just as building the scene was your job, so is this. It's a kind of symbolic reconnecting with the time and place in which we started – the group room on a Tuesday evening. So, if you are ready perhaps you could take each person back to their seat and put the chairs back where you got them from then we'll do some sharing.'

When the group came back together in a circle, Jo invited the people who had played a role in the recreation of Pink Bay to say something about the experience. Bob spoke of how strong, serene and silent he had felt as the old raft bobbing about in the sea; Sarah spoke of her delight in the strength of the tree and what pleasure she had felt in reaching up towards the sunlight while people clustered at her base seeking protection; Louise (who had been a seagull) told of the freedom she had felt swooping above the waves. Everybody who had held a role told Sandra something about how they had felt in that role.

When sharing from role was complete, Jo invited the group to tell Sandra about the connections with their own lives brought up by the recreation of Pink Bay. The tales told were of childhood pleasures, beach holidays, delight in the sun, but also about the sadness of separation and loss. Jo and Pete too

*shared what they had been reminded of by their journey with
Sandra to Pink Bay.*

Although still some way off a complete psychodrama enaction,
the story of Pink Bay introduces many elements of psychodrama
beside the creation of a scene. Sandra was a protagonist and had
some limited experience of role reversal as she took the parts of
the elements of her scene. She experienced the world as, for
example, an old swimming raft, a seagull and a tree. Other members of the group became auxiliaries for the first time and there
was an introduction to the formality of psychodrama sharing –
sharing first from role (both as a way of de-roling and to give the
protagonist more information about the enaction) and then from
personal experience, making connections with the protagonist
without analysing or offering a critique of the enaction.

Other elements of psychodrama can be introduced in similar
ways. For example, a group may be introduced to the idea of role
reversal by inviting each person to think of someone they know
well and to take on the characteristics of this person, their
mannerisms, their way of walking, sitting and standing as well as
the way in which they speak.

*It was the third session of the group and they had been
together for about twenty minutes when Jane, the group
leader said, 'Last week we did some scene-setting. Frank took
us all to that stone circle up on the moors and we had
Christmas dinner at Philippa's house. This week I thought
you might like a go at role reversal. Role reversal is the bit of
psychodrama when the person whose drama it is becomes
someone or something else in it. Perhaps you become your
mum or your chest of drawers – anything really. It's different
from being an auxiliary, which all of you were at some point
last week, because you are playing a part in your own
drama, not somebody else's.*

*'What I would like you to do is to think of someone you
know well, a friend, someone in your family, someone you
know at work or socially and then you're going to have the
chance to become them for a little while.*

*'When you have thought of someone, take a few moments to
imagine how they sit, stand and walk around and then give
that a go – walk around the room as if you were this person.*

If you like, when you pass somebody you can do what you think they would do. Go on then – give it a go!'

The group members sat for a while thinking, one or two of them looking quite uncertain. Eventually they began to move around the room. Some shuffled, some strode boldly, chests out – for others differences in gait from their own were more subtle.

After a few minutes, Jane said, 'OK, if you haven't already you can stop now. What I'd like you to do is to find a partner and, in your pairs, to take it in turns to talk like the person you have chosen – or you could choose another if you like. It doesn't matter what you talk about – it could even be the weather – but it might work better if you talk about something your person might really be interested in. When you are in the listening role, just respond as yourself. You have fifteen minutes. I'll tell you when you are half-way through.'

When time was up, Jane asked the group members to pull their chairs into a circle and invited them to tell what it was like to be this other person.

'It was really strange,' said Kim. 'I was my old boyfriend and it wasn't until I started to sit like him when I was talking to Sheila that I realized just how nervous he is. All the time we were going out together, and I never knew!'

'I was my boss,' said George, 'and when Phil asked me if I liked what I did, I said "No" straight away. I'm sure that's right but if you had asked me earlier on if my boss liked what he does for a living I would have said yes. Where did that come from I wonder?'

Others in the group shared about the insights they had found into the lives and inner worlds of the people they had been. They also all agreed that taking on the role of somebody else was easier than they had thought.

Vignettes (brief, mini-psychodramas) can also be useful when introducing a new group to psychodrama. Luxmore (1995: 6) writes:

Because they are, by definition, briefer than classical psychodrama enactments, vignettes can be particularly useful at the start of a group's lifetime. Their necessary brevity can have the effect of allowing apprehensive group members to try out important aspects of psychodrama – scene-setting and role reversal for example – without feeling that they are taking on more than they are yet ready for. Vignettes can introduce group members to psychodrama techniques as well as being a way of introducing members of a group to each other's worlds: 'This is my kitchen, where I spend most of my time.'

A *vignette* is a contained enactment, exploring a single scene and perhaps involving only a protagonist and one auxiliary (exceptionally more, and sometimes none). It is often a dialogue between the protagonist and another person (or perhaps another aspect of the protagonist). The role of the other may be held by another group member or it may be that an empty chair serves the function. Usually, a vignette is time-limited, the director and the protagonist agreeing that they will work together for perhaps twenty minutes (psychodrama proper may last an hour or even two) and there is a specific objective. This could be to address unfinished business with someone, to say what was not said. The scene-building tends not to be as elaborate as when a full psychodrama is anticipated.

In the simplest form of vignette, the protagonist is invited to place two chairs in such a way as there can be some kind of interaction between whosoever will be occupying them. One of these chairs is for the protagonist, the second for the other person involved in the dialogue. Vignettes offer many opportunities for role reversal and, if the director and the protagonist wish it, for spontaneous doubling. The story of Michael talking to his brother told in Chapter 2 is an example of a vignette.

5

THE FIRST SCENE: MOVING INTO ACTION

The Importance of 'Encounter' and Group Process

In a group familiar with psychodrama, sessions tend to follow a similar pattern. First, there is a process of coming together. This may simply be an opportunity to 'check in', that is, a few moments in which each member of the group can say how they are and tell of any significant events in their lives, but it may also be a time in which group issues are addressed. Psychodrama is a *group* approach to psychotherapy and personal growth not simply a set of action techniques. Group process is an important part of psychodrama and relationships between group members (including group leaders) can often be addressed directly and in the present. This process of encounter, in both a Morenian and a Rogerian (see Rogers, 1970) sense, is a meeting of the real self of one person with the real self of another. It is much more than emotional self-disclosure, and although conflict may occur, it is not deliberately provoked. Encounter is less about emotional release and 'sorting things out' than about risking saying or showing 'This is me' and asking 'Who are you?' with the intention to understand. Catharsis and conflict resolution may be a result of this process but more as a by-product than as an objective. The objectives of encounter are increased self-acceptance, authenticity, openness to others, enhanced spontaneity and a realization of innate creativity.

In psychodrama, *encounter* is sometimes defined in relation only to enactment – that is, as the process which occurs when an individual truly meets with significant others on the psychodramatic stage. Regardless of the time in which this action is set, encounter *always* takes place in the present. However, 'encounter' can just as validly be applied to the process of interaction between group members in the 'here-and-now' of the psychodrama session. This emphasis on the present is fundamental to psychodrama. Blatner (1997: xvi–xvii) records that Moreno coined the term 'here-and-now', and Hare and Hare (1996: 36) write: 'The encounter happens in *the moment*, in the *here-and-now* . . . Encounter is the real basis of the psychotherapeutic process, although transference and counter-transference may be imposed upon it.'

Writing about psychodrama, Corey (1994: 209) points out that encounter is a process by which 'people not only meet but also understand each other on a deep and significant level' and that 'it fosters a sense of community in a group, which builds the trust that is necessary for productive work'. This trust and under-standing will arise out of psychodramatic work itself when a group is functioning well but it can also be the product of the direct engagement of group members with each other and the director. It is also true that, denied other outlets, group issues particularly those to do with relationships between group members and group members and the director, will tend to emerge on the psychodrama stage. Psychodramatists take different views as to the extent to which this is desirable. Some prefer to concentrate on enactment as a way of addressing group issues and others see separate attention to relationships in the group as conducive to good psychodrama and a 'rush to action' at the expense of group process as counter-productive. Sometimes encounter and psycho-dramatic enaction can go hand in hand. For example, Williams (1989: 187–190), with reference to clinical example, shows how they may be used together to address issues between a group member and the director, and Luxmore (1995: 15) discusses the usefulness of vignettes in addressing group process. He writes:

> The usefulness of a vignette as a means of clarification is one way of addressing group issues. Where talking directly across the room to another group member feels too dangerous to do, a vignette can enable the protagonist to talk to his or her *perception* of that group member using an empty chair and role reversal, thereby clarifying not only what needs to be said but the difference between the perceived and the actual person.

What is certain is that if the real relationships within the group are ignored or neglected, then the psychodramatic work will tend to occur only on a superficial level if it occurs at all. It may not matter *how* group issues are dealt with (although psychodramatists will have their preferred methods and differences of rationale), but it is essential that they are.

Warming-up

The warm-up is the first of the three elements of a classical psychodrama (the other two are enactment and sharing). Blatner (1997: 42) writes 'to warm up to an activity is to become gradually more spontaneous and involved'. The process of warming up to psychodrama is one of becoming present in the room, centring on the group, developing a sense of trust in the leader and the others present, becoming more receptive to intuition, imagination, emotion without neglecting rational thought, engendering a spirit of playfulness and becoming increasingly prepared to take risks, to encounter people, places, ideas and things in a new way. There is also a parallel with the notion of warming up in, for example, athletics and dance, because a psychodrama warm-up often has a physical component. It can be about moving and 'doing' as a way of energy-raising and awakening the body-sense on which psychodrama relies. Jonathan Moreno (1994: 106–107), explaining the potency of a psychodrama warm-up in comparison to '"talk therapy" alone' states, 'engagement in overt bodily activity vastly increases the protagonist's affective involvement in the subject matter.'

Before facilitating the warming up of the group, psychodramatists have a responsibility to warm themselves up. The group leader's warm-up is an opportunity to raise energy and to focus on the group and the task ahead. It is time to reflect upon the possibilities the group offers and the hitches and snags which may arise. Perhaps most importantly it is a time for group leaders to take stock of themselves *before* meeting with the clients. For example, is there anything in the personal life of the group leader that needs to be addressed, bracketed off or disclosed at an early stage in order to facilitate good functioning? How does the leader feel about this group? What prejudices and preconceptions may get in the way of encountering the group members? Is there an urge to 'perform', entertain, drive for action, or is the group leader able to 'go with the flow', perhaps even accepting that there may not be anything particularly 'dramatic' about the forthcoming session? A well-prepared psychodramatist will have addressed some or all of this in supervision prior to the group meeting but it never hurts to run an internal check. Talking things over with a co-therapist too can be helpful – this is also an opportunity for the co-therapy team to warm up to each other.

Another Thursday evening. Bill was on his way to the rented room in the local community centre where he and Jean held their regular psychodrama group. He would arrive there about 20 minutes before the group was due to start. As he walked, he thought about the events of his day and the session to come. He entered the building and turned towards the kitchen – Jean was already there and, Heaven be praised, already had the kettle on.

As they sat with their mugs of tea, Bill and Jean talked. First they spoke of nothing in particular, mutual friends and acquaintances, what had happened at work that day, the events of the last week, whatever came to mind. Gradually, their conversation became more focused on psychodrama and the group. Bill had rowed with his daughter. He told Jean about this both because he needed to talk about it, to process it for himself, and because there were a number of young women of a similar age to his daughter in the group. He wanted to be clear that he could separate his relationship with his daughter from his relationships in the group and he wanted Jean to know as an additional safeguard. Jean listened in her attentive and accepting way. As usual, she didn't say much but, also as usual, Bill found his head and heart clearer as a result. They then talked a bit about the group members, wondering how the threads from last week would be picked up that evening. Who might wish to be protagonist, how they felt about directing, which group members seemed vulnerable or needy and so on.

When they had finished their tea, Bill and Jean went into the group room. It was still about five minutes before the group was due to start but they liked to take a little time just to get the feel of the space. They rearranged the furniture so that they and the group could sit together and so that there would be plenty of room for any psychodrama enactment which might occur. This was preparation, familiarization and, importantly, an act of transformation, turning the room from its daytime function into a space 'owned' by Jean, Bill and the rest of the group. As the group members began to enter the room, Bill and Jean smiled at each other and took their seats. They both felt focused, trusting of each other and ready to begin.

The psychodramatist's warm-up continues as the group assembles and the session starts. Physical activity may be an important part of this, as may be an element of playfulness. 'Play' has a serious function in psychodrama. Bradbury (1995a: 22), in a paper addressing the importance of play in psychodrama and as an agent of therapeutic change, writes:

> Play is a fundamental capacity of humans which provides access to the inner world where psychodramatic investigation can occur. It is also the seed bed in which the changes consequent on psychotherapeutic interventions occur. Within this, it is spontaneity and creativity which provide the trust towards growth.

The psychodramatist's playfulness is not only part of the personal warm-up but it also facilitates the playfulness of group members. Blatner (1997: 44) discusses the director's warm-up and points out the importance of modelling, including 'some of the elements directly associated with psychodrama, such as physical movement or shifting a chair's position'. Some element of self-disclosure can also usefully be part of the psychodramatist's warm-up. This is in part about modelling, partly about centring and becoming present and partly about offering the group some insight into its leader. Blatner (1997: 44) has pointed out the importance of this element in the warming up of the other group members:

> What people really need to know is how judgmental, shaming, authoritarian, mutual, flexible, playful, non-defensive, and in other ways comfortable the director will be . . . so, during her [*sic*] own warm-up, the director discloses some of her own style.

Casson (1997b: 4), pointing out that Moreno calls for a real relationship between therapist and client, echoes this: 'some transparency, immediacy, presence, warmth, sharing from the therapist can enable this to be established.' It is this willingness of the psychodramatist to be real in the encounter which enables tele, the process of mutual appreciation and understanding upon which psychodrama depends.

As psychodramatists model, disclose, walk around the room, play etc. as part of their warm-up, so the group starts to warm. Sharing something of the events of the week is part of the warm-up but there are many other ways in which psychodramatists warm up groups. Blatner (1997: 47) distinguishes between undirected and directed warm-ups. Checking in is an example of the former, as is an encounter session and, in groups who know each other well, this opportunity to talk together, share feelings, laugh, joke, cry, complain and argue is often enough to warm a group up to action. This may also be the preferred warm-up method of the group leader; for example, in person-centred psychodrama, action often emerges from group process. What happens in the encounter between group members is the spur to act hunger and the identification of a protagonist.

In directed warm-ups some stimulus or suggestion comes from the psychodramatist. This might be in the form of a sociometric exercise, a game, an invitation to use art materials to express a mood, place or time, a guided fantasy, listening to or making music or dancing, amongst other things. The introductory exercises described in Chapter 4 could equally well be used as directed warm-ups for a more established group. Many of the techniques of dramatherapy can be used as psychodrama warm-ups, but there is a difference of intent. In psychodrama, games and exercises, if they are used at all, are to prepare a group for action and to identify a protagonist. In dramatherapy, growth and healing arise from drama processes *per se*. The exercise, game or activity is a form of dramatic projection through which, writes Jones (1996: 7), 'the client becomes emotionally and intellectually involved in encountering [problematic areas] in dramatic forms such as characters, play materials or puppets'.

Psychodramatists may introduce an idea of their own as the focus for a directed warm-up but it is more likely that their suggestions will relate to group process or to an issue previously raised in the group but not dealt with or resolved.

Jim looked around the group and said, 'Last week lots of us were talking about our identity, who we were, where we were from, who was like us, who was different. I've been thinking a bit about that since and, if you would like to, I have an idea which might help us take that a bit further. Something for us all to do and perhaps for someone to take a bit further as a protagonist. What do you think?'

'What do you mean?' asked Heather.

'Yeah – I guess it would be fairer to tell you more before I asked you to commit yourselves,' replied Jim. 'What I had in mind was for each of us to make some kind of representation of ourselves and to share that with the group. I've brought a

*tin full of pebbles with me. I thought it might be useful for us
to use them to make a picture of ourselves. Different rocks
could be different parts of us or perhaps the people around
us. Or you could use something you've brought with you. Just
as we have sculpted the group using ourselves and things in
the room, this would be an opportunity to sculpt ourselves.'*

The group thought it was a good idea and, as Jim opened
the tin of pebbles, there was an almost unseemly rush to grab
them. Group members went to their private spaces within the
room and with a quiet intensity set about modelling themselves.

When everyone was finished, Jim invited them to share
with the group what they had made, naming the elements
and to say as much or as little about their sculpts as they
wished.

Brian offered to start. His sculpture comprised six pebbles
and his house keys. *'This big one at the front'*, he said, *'is the
bit of me the world sees. I like it because it is big, solid and
full of all sorts of colours and shapes. That's a bit like how I
like to be seen. I've put my keys in the front row too – I'm not
sure why. I thought it was because they represented my house
– house, home they are important things to me. But keys can
be about security too can't they? Perhaps that is what they
mean. The bit of me that needs to feel secure – and home is
where I feel secure, grounded, rooted. Yeah, that sounds
right.*

*'Also in the front row is this funny knobbly rock with all
the holes. This is the bit of me that can be funny – both funny
ha–ha and funny peculiar. It is my odd, eccentric bit – I
know you've all seen it! Behind the big pebble I started with is
a smaller pebble. That is me how I feel inside. I thought at
first it was different from the one in front but, when I looked
more closely I realized that it too is full of many colours and
shapes – a bit brighter and a bit more subtle – if that makes
sense. So that has got me wondering. Am I really the same
outwardly as I am inwardly even though I think I'm hiding?
I think that is probably right too.*

*'Off to the side is this lovely bit of sparkly quartz. See how
it shines in the light? I like this translucent creamy white
and that hint of pink. This is about being brilliant. I don't
mean intellectually – I mean dazzling, putting others off by
shining a light in their eyes. When this bit of me is in the*

lead, people can't really see me – things just bounce off. I've chosen a smaller rock for this than I would have a little while ago. It isn't such a big part of me now.

'This one towards the back,' said Brian, pointing to a small, matt-black pebble, 'is my shadow side. It is dark, hidden away. I don't think it is evil and it too is smaller now than it used to be . . . but it is still there. Sometimes it frightens me because I don't know what is in it.

'Right at the very back is this beautiful cream stone. I don't know why I've put it there. It seemed the right thing to do. I've been looking at it a lot. It looks vaguely heart-shaped to me. I wonder if that means anything?'

*Brian paused and looked lost in thought. The group waited, attentive in their silence. 'I don't know,' said Brian at last. 'It **does** mean something but I can't get it at the moment.'*

There was another pause and then Brian opened his hand to reveal a small pebble. 'This is the small part of me,' he said. Closing his hand again, he continued, 'I don't mind you seeing it – in fact it is rather nice to show you – but not for too long. I want to keep it safely in my hand.

'That's me,' he said. 'Somebody else now.'

Each member of the group shared what they had made with the pebbles. The interpretation each of them had put upon the exercise was different but everyone took the opportunity to share with the group something about how they saw them- selves, how they were in the world or how others saw them. In sharing, many connections were made with the sculptures of others but most of the group said something to Brian. Some shared that they too had a shadow side of which they were fearful and almost everybody identified with the small part of Brian which had to be looked after and protected.

Identifying a Protagonist

As well as promoting group cohesion and trust, raising energy and preparing everybody to participate in a psychodrama enactment, warm-ups may be the means by which a protagonist is identified. Karp (1995: 296) describes how different forms of warm-up may be used to select a protagonist:

Moreno [warmed a group up] by 'encountering' everyone and getting people to talk easily to each other. A person who had a theme was accepted by the group as their protagonist. Another way is for the director to select a protagonist, one whom she thinks is ready to work. Another alternative is through creative group exercise from which the subject of the session emerges. This is called a protagonist-centred warm-up. In a self-nomination warm-up, people can put themselves forward to be the subject.

Blatner (1997: 52–57) lists some of the ways in which a protagonist may emerge from group process. These include:

1   A protagonist may volunteer or have previously volunteered in an earlier session.
2   The protagonist may be preselected by the therapists.
3   Group leaders may talk to individuals in the group until they find someone who is ready to be protagonist.
4   The group leader may 'give a short talk on some theme, tell a story that seems relevant to the group's interest' in the hope that this stimulates the group to explore some issue. As a result, a protagonist may volunteer.
5   The protagonist may emerge out of the on-going group process. If group leaders facilitate the conversation and interaction of the group, perhaps participating themselves, then 'eventually both a theme and a protagonist emerge'.
6   Using sociometric techniques, sociodrama or other group-centred methods, a protagonist may emerge as one who is especially concerned about something triggered in the discussion.

Sometimes, whatever the nature of the warm-up, selecting a protagonist is simple because only one person expresses the desire to take that role, the group is clearly in sympathy with the issue to be explored and supportive of the prospective protagonist and the psychodramatist is ready and able to work with the issue and the person. For example, after the exercise with pebbles described above, when Jim asked if anyone wished to take their exploration further, Brian was the only person who offered to be protagonist. It was clear that the group were deeply involved with Brian's story and very willing to help in this exploration. Jim too was inclined to work with Brian as protagonist. Brian's drama started with a scene in which the elements of his sculpture were represented by group members. When there is more than one potential protagonist, the group and the director has to find a way of choosing between them.

When more than one potential protagonist declares themselves, there are three major options for choosing between them. The choice can be made by the group, by discussion between the potential protagonists or by the psychodramatist. However the choice is made, it is essential that it is with the approval and support of the group. For this reason many psychodramatists prefer a method of protagonist selection which is open, in which potential protagonists are encouraged to say something about the issue they wish to explore and in which any decisions taken by the director are explained and perhaps even open to question. A common way of choosing between potential protagonists in a traditional approach to psychodrama is by way of a sociometric version of a group vote.

The group had been talking of mothers, fathers and families for a little while when Christine, the group leader asked if anyone wanted to take what they had been talking about into action. Pat, Tom and Rose had all expressed the desire to be protagonist. Christine invited them all into the central space. 'I would like you to sit down, facing each other and then to tell us what it is you want to work on and maybe a little about why. I don't want you to go too far into things – just say enough so that the rest of us can get a clear idea of what your drama might be about. When you have all done that, I will ask the rest of the group to choose which psychodrama they are most interested in.'

Rose went first, telling the group that she wanted to do something about her relationship with her mother. Pat wanted to look at her tendency to flare up angrily at her children, sometimes when they did not really deserve it. Tom's story was about his difficulty in expressing the soft side of his nature and how this seemed to interfere when he tried to relate to his children.

'OK,' Christine said to the rest of the group, 'you have heard what Rose, Pat and Tom have to say. Now I would like you to go and sit behind the one whose psychodrama you feel most drawn to at the moment. You can do this intuitively, spontaneously – in fact that might work best. If you don't know, just go and stand or sit behind each one and see what feelings come up for you. You'll probably know then. Remember, you are not really choosing between the people, you are choosing the story – perhaps it has most meaning for you in this moment, perhaps you have more energy for it, I don't know . . . but you will.

> *'The person with the most supporters will be our protago-*
> *nist today but before we move into action the other two will*
> *get a chance to tell us a bit more about their issue and why it*
> *is important to them.'*
>
> *Some group members went instantly to one of the potential*
> *protagonists, some moved from one to the other testing out*
> *their sympathies. When everybody had made a choice, Chris-*
> *tine said, 'Rose has three people with her, Pat has two and*
> *Tom has four. OK Tom, I guess you are our protagonist today*
> *but before we start, I'd like Rose and Pat to say more about*
> *their reasons for offering to be protagonist. Those of you who*
> *have chosen them, stay with them while they tell their stories.*
> *Rose and Pat, you each have about ten minutes to tell us why*
> *you wanted to work today. Who wants to go first?*
>
> *Rose and Pat each told more of their stories and then Tom's*
> *psychodrama began.*

Rarely, the group leader will decline a group member's offer to be a protagonist. There are three major reasons why this may happen. First, the psychodramatist may feel that they are limited in some way, not warmed up enough to the issue or the potential protagonist. Second, the group may not be ready to move to action and/or be out of sympathy with the potential protagonist. This may require that more time be spent attending to group process. Lastly, the psychodramatist may decide that for the potential protagonist to work on the declared issue at this time would be counter-therapeutic. Amongst other things, this judge-ment may be about the extent to which the protagonist is engaged with the issue – perhaps there is no real evidence of act hunger, it may be in response to a sense that the group would become alienated from the action and therefore from the protagonist, it may be that the psychodramatist senses that re-enactment would be damaging.

Choosing the Director

When two psychodramatists work together as co-therapists, there is a choice of director for any enactment. In some working relationships it is the psychodramatists who choose which of them will direct, perhaps deciding before the group starts and announc-ing their decision at an early stage and specifically before a potential protagonist is declared. Sometimes this choice is made by the co-therapists in response to the protagonist selected – the psychodramatist most warmed-up to the issue and to the protagonist offering to direct – or sometimes the choice is on a turn-taking basis. Other co-therapists encourage the protagonist to choose which of them is to be director. When I work with a co-therapist, whichever of us has facilitated the identification of the protagonist asks 'Which of us would you like to direct?' as the final act of this process. The person chosen then proceeds to scene-setting, the selection of auxiliaries and the direction of action and sharing.

Group members base their choice of director on many things. The most frequently mentioned reason for the choice made is the director's gender or that the protagonist sensed that one or other of the co-therapists was in some way more sympathetic. Often, this seems to be about tele, that is, about the real relationship in the present and a sense of mutual understanding, but it can also have some reference to the protagonist's previous relationships. The latter can embrace the notion of transference. Group members also often take account of who directed the last psychodrama and choose the other co-therapist. Most often, this means that protagonists who have a strong preference will wait until they are sure that it is the turn of the director they want before declaring themselves. Sometimes one of the co-therapists is chosen to direct because the protagonist wants the other to be an auxiliary in the drama.

The Beginnings of the Enactment

When both protagonist and director have been chosen, they work together to define the issue, establish the first scene and populate it with auxiliaries. The immediate task is to determine the starting point from which, through several scenes, a psychodrama may unfold. Normally, the director will move towards the protagonist, perhaps sitting by them or in some other way symbolically demonstrating the developing working alliance. Physical proximity also allows greater empathy and for the director to pick up on the body (or kinaesthetic) signals. All of this strengthens the bond between protagonist and director and gives the latter more invitation on which to base suggestions and invitations.

In the opening minutes of the psychodrama the director may restate the protagonist's issue. This is both about directors checking their perceptions ('This is what I think you said. Have I got it right?') and a reminder to the rest of the group. Sometimes there is value in the protagonist taking a few minutes to talk about what they wish to explore; this provides the group with more information and centres the protagonist on the task to hand, but usually the director will issue an early invitation to action ('Don't tell us, show us').

> 'You said that you wanted to do something about your relationship with your sister,' said Jennifer to Molly, 'Something about the fact that, ever since your mum died she doesn't seem to want to talk to you. You don't know why that is and it makes you sad. Have I got that right?'
>
> 'Yes,' said Molly. 'She was so important to me when we were growing up and I miss her. I'd really like to sort out what has gone wrong between us.'
>
> 'As you speak, I can feel your sadness,' said Jennifer. 'Do you know how you would like to start?'
>
> 'Not really,' replied Molly. 'I feel really stuck about it all.'
>
> 'I guess that's right – you are stuck,' said Jennifer. 'Could that be a place to start – with the stuckness?'
>
> 'I don't know – I'm feeling more and more stuck,' said Molly gloomily.
>
> 'OK,' said Jennifer rising to her feet. 'Can we see what happens if we move into the space – perhaps if we just walk around a bit while you tell us something about your sister or being stuck or something.' They moved into the working space together and began to walk side by side.
>
> After a short while, Molly said, 'Perhaps if I could talk to Vera – that's my sister – I could ask her what this is all about.'
>
> 'OK,' said Jennifer. 'Where would you like to do that?'
>
> 'What about the front room in my parent's old house – the one we grew up in? We had some good times there and when I think about it I remember how close we used to be,' Molly said.
>
> 'The front room in your parent's old house,' said Jennifer. 'That seems the right place for you to start? OK, can you show us what it was like?'

When the protagonist has a starting point, which may be a moment, a place, an encounter or some combination of these, the director's next task is to assist in the process of scene-setting. Using the things (and sometimes the people) in the group room,

78

the protagonist makes a representation of the place where the action is to start. Sometimes the protagonist finds this easy and moves rapidly to move the furniture in the room into new positions on what is or has become the psychodrama stage.

'This is my sitting room,' said Suzy, dragging one of the chairs into the working space, 'and this is my armchair – I sit here while I sew, watch the tele, relax. The television is over there,' she said pointing to the corner as she moved another chair. 'That table will do for that. There's another armchair over here. Now I need something to be the coffee table. That stool will do,' she said moving it to the right position. Working rapidly, Suzy moved more tables and chairs until she had made the room to her satisfaction. Eventually she paused and looked thoughtfully at her scene.

'Is there anything else?' asked June, the director.

'No – no, I don't think so,' was the reply. 'Oh – wait a minute – there's the standard lamp. Me and Graham bought that together in the local flea market when we were first married. How could I have forgotten that?'

'Do you need the standard lamp?' asked June.

'Yes – yes I do,' said Suzy.

'OK – what could be the standard lamp?' enquired June.

'I can't see anything that looks right – can I have a person? Robert is so tall and thin he would be perfect,' said Suzy.

'Yes, you can have a person. Is that all right, Robert?' said June. Robert nodded.

'Sure,' he said.

'Before Robert comes into your sitting room Suzy could you go and be the standard lamp? Show us where it is in the room?' June asked. Suzy went and stood beside the first chair she had put in the scene, her chair. 'Right,' said June, 'you are the standard lamp in Suzy's sitting room. What three words would you use to describe yourself, standard lamp?'

'I'm tall, stronger than I look and – er – I'm precious,' said the standard lamp, in a slightly surprised voice.

'OK, Robert – is that enough to start?' asked June.

'Yes – tall, strong and precious,' said Robert.

'Stronger than you look,' reminded June.

'Right, standard lamp, can you become Suzy again and Robert can you go and become the standard lamp,' said June. 'Is that everything now Suzy?'

Suzy said that it was and she and June moved on to identify and enrol the auxiliaries she would need for her drama.

Sometimes the protagonist needs more help from the director to establish the scene. This may involve aiding the protagonist to build up a mental picture of the setting before moving on to represent it in the room. Asking a protagonist to recall the sights, sounds and smells of the scene may be very helpful. From this gradually built up but vividly recalled picture, protagonist and director can move on to making a physical representation of it as described above.

Auxiliaries and Doubles

When the physical elements of a scene are in place, it is time to introduce the people who are present in it. These are the auxiliaries. Normal practice now is that the protagonist chooses people to be auxiliaries from the other members of the group. There is an assumption that, through the telic process, the protagonist will choose the best person for the role, that is, the person most likely to play the part in the required way. Directors encourage protagonists to select their auxiliaries in an intuitive way. Although sometimes the gender, age, physical appearance etc. of the auxiliary may be important, often it is not and the protagonist is advised to choose the person who, to them, instinctively feels right for the role regardless of their apparent attributes. In psychodrama, there is no reason at all why a taciturn, grey-haired and bearded grandfather cannot play the role of an effervescent, ebullient, extrovert girl child if that is who the protagonist spontaneously chooses. Some essential quality will have been recognized.

Although the protagonist is normally given a free choice in choosing auxiliaries, it is important that the person chosen has the right of refusal. Sometimes too the director may interfere with the choice of auxiliaries either by restricting that choice at the outset or intervening when someone is selected. When this happens, it is most commonly because the director is aware that for the person chosen to carry the role would be detrimental to the individual, the protagonist or the group. For example, as a psychodrama trainee, I took part in a weekend session in which gender issues were very much part of the group process. When one of the women put herself forward as protagonist and declared that she wished to work on the issue of her abusive relationships with men, although I was very willing for her to do this, my heart sank. I thought to myself, 'Here we go again, another abusive man role for at least one of us.' I felt fearful, reluctant but ultimately resigned. I didn't want to be chosen as auxiliary but, if chosen, I would have done my best. My sense was that the other men in the group were going through a similar process. Later, I found out that this was true. To my enormous relief, as the protagonist moved on to the stage, the director said that she wanted the protagonist to have women to play all the parts in the drama. The director said that this was principally because for women to take the parts of abusive men would result in a more meaningful drama (women are sometimes better at playing aggressive, rude and violent men because they are less concerned about confusion between themselves and the role than are men) and because she thought that, if men played those parts there was a danger that the protagonist's issue would be obscured or muddied by group issues. I think too it was an act of kindness. The director had picked up on the war-weariness of the men. Whatever the reasons, this was a very successful psychodrama, the women auxiliaries were able to be present for the protagonist in a way which would have been very difficult for the men in the group.

However they are chosen, auxiliaries are enabled in their tasks as 'significant others' in the protagonist's psychodrama by the protagonist and director working together to give them the information they will need to carry the role. Most commonly this is done by role reversal, the director asks the protagonist to take the auxiliary role to show how that person is to be in the drama. Sometimes the director will interview the protagonist-as-auxiliary, sometimes an invitation to provide any significant information is extended and sometimes a short description is requested. When either the director or the protagonist judges or intuitively senses this to be too difficult, perhaps because of intense conflict between the protagonist and the person to be represented by the auxiliary, then the protagonist may be asked to double the auxiliary role, for example by standing behind a chair on which the auxiliary will sit, speaking in the first person but at 'arm's length'. This preserves a necessary element of distance and allows the protagonist to give information about the role without becoming swamped by it. Auxiliaries can be chosen before or after the protagonist has role-reversed or doubled the role. If the protagonist is asked to select the auxiliary first, then the person chosen has the opportunity to pay particular attention to the protagonist's version of the person they are to play. If this comes second, then at the time of choosing, the protagonist is more warmed up to the role and so is the audience from whom the auxiliary will be chosen. This can be seen as enhancing tele. Some directors have a strong attachment to one process or the other, many use whichever seems appropriate at the time. Once in role and on the stage, an auxiliary's job is to use their sense of that role and their own spontaneity to respond to the protagonist. This is less about getting it 'right' and more a case of trusting the psychodramatic process, the instinct of the protagonist in choosing the auxiliary and the prompting of the auxiliary's intuition. A good rule for auxiliaries is, if a word, phrase or action pops into your head while in role, do it or say it even if you do not understand its relevance or where it came from, the chances are that it will be appropriate. Auxiliaries are not required to be perfect – the director will from time to time check with the protagonist that the auxiliary is doing and saying the right things and, if they are not, the protagonist will be invited to role-reverse to show how things should be done. In my experience as a director, the response I get most frequently to that question is, 'Yes – that's right – that's exactly how they would say that.'

Diane was going to meet psychodramatically with two of her old school friends. She had set the scene in the park where, as young teenagers, they had spent so much time. There were trees, acres of grass and two park benches, one each side of a pathway. This meeting was taking place after school. It was Diane's memory of a real event.

'Right Diane,' said Julie, 'You said that you wanted to start by talking to your two friends. Is it time for us to meet them?' Diane nodded. 'OK. Who are we going to meet first? Who do you want to bring into the scene first?' asked Julie.

'Anita,' replied Diane.

'OK – could you be Anita for a little while? Put yourself in the park as she is going to be in this scene?' requested Julie. Diane walked over to one of the two benches and flopped down at one end. Julie moved towards her: 'Hello, Anita,' she said. 'Diane tells me you're a good friend of hers – is that right?'

'Yeah – Di's great – she's a real laugh.'

'Have you known her long?' asked Julie.

'We were at primary school together and we've been friends ever since. We're nearly the same age you know so we have joint birthday parties. Next year we'll be fifteen and it's going to be in a club – but we haven't told our mums yet!'

'You seem quite mischievous Anita – is that right?'

'Well – I can be – but I have a serious side too. It's usually me who insists that we do our homework – we do it together me, Di and Jo – she's our mate.'

'So you can be serious as well as mischievous and the three of you seem quite close. Is that right and is there anything else we should know about you, Anita?' asked Julie.

'We are **very** close. I like dancing and I'm good at maths and I'm going to go to university after school – to Aberdeen because that's as far away from home as I can get.'

'Thank you, Anita. Can you reverse roles, become Diane again and come over here with me?' said Julie. As Diane left the scene and became herself once more, Julie said, 'Now we've met Anita I wonder who you would like to be her in your drama? Just look around the group and pick the person who feels right to you.'

Diane looked around the group. 'Debbie – will you be Anita please?' she asked.

'Is that all right, Debbie, and if so is there anything else you need to know about Anita?' said Julie.

'Yes – that's fine. What do I look like?' replied Debbie.

'You're a bit skinny, long dark hair and long legs, big brown eyes,' said Diane.

'Right, Debbie come and sit on the park bench and be Anita. Who else do we need Diane?' asked Julie.

'Jo's here too – shall I go and be her?' Diane said.

'Yes – that's a good idea,' said Julie.

Julie interviewed Diane as Jo in a similar way as she had Anita. Reversing back into her own role, Diane chose Billie to play the part of Jo.

'We have Anita and we have Jo. Was anybody else present at the time?' Julie asked. 'Umm – let me think. There was someone sitting on the other bench. Do you think that's important?' enquired Diane.

'I don't know. What do you think? Would you like to have someone in that role? I guess the fact that you've remembered may mean something,' Julie said.

'Yeah – well. It was an old guy – well he looked old to us then. I guess he was about forty. We didn't talk to him and he didn't say anything to us but he was there, reading his newspaper.'

'Right,' said Julie. 'You don't know whether or not he is important but he was there so perhaps he should be here. I guess we have nothing to lose by including him? No? OK, then perhaps you could go over to the other bench and show us how he was sitting. Do you need something to be the newspaper?'

Diane picked up a book and went over to the other bench, sitting down but remaining in an upright posture with her legs crossed. 'I'm just sitting here reading my paper, enjoying this peaceful afternoon. Those giggly girls have just arrived but they aren't really bothering me. I can hear them though.'

'Hello, Man on the Bench,' said Julie. 'Do you have a name?'

'No,' was the brusque reply.

'OK, can you please tell us three things about yourself?' Julie requested.

'I'm absorbed and quiet – but I don't miss much.'

At Julie's suggestion, Diane reversed out of the role of Man on the Bench and chose Malcolm to be her auxiliary. Diane entered the scene as her fourteen-year-old self, sitting between Anita and Jo and the action began.

When a protagonist finds it hard to express thoughts and feelings or feels in need of support to enter the scene at all, the director may suggest that they choose someone to be their double. In this context a double (also called a supportive or permanent double) is a particular kind of auxiliary – in effect playing the parts of the protagonist which are too difficult for the protagonist themselves. The double's job can include duplicating the non-verbal expression of the protagonist and using this as a clue to what isn't being said. In this and in other ways, the double tunes in to what isn't being expressed and says or in some other way expresses it as if they were the protagonist. Karp (1995: 295) illustrates this well:

Because Moreno felt that the royal route to the psyche is not the word but non-verbal expression, the auxiliary ego can express, by gesture, posture or distance, those unspoken secrets in relation to the protagonist. I was once a double for a man who was having a quite normal dinner conversation with his wife of twenty years. He was telling her he didn't like to eat liver and clenched his fist as he spoke. As his double, I also clenched my fist and went a step further. I slammed my fist down on the table and said, 'I've had enough of not being understood, I want a divorce.' He looked at me, shocked, and said to her, 'So do I!' It was the non-verbal clue that spoke the truth, not his words. His body conveyed the truth while his words masked it. He then chose to express his actual feelings.

Doubles are chosen by protagonists in a similar way to which they would choose any other auxiliary.

When the scene is set and the auxiliaries are on stage, the protagonist and director enter the scene and the enactment can begin.

6

THE SECOND SCENE: ENACTMENT

The Director's Inspiration

The core of psychodrama is the enactment, indeed if someone talks about 'a psychodrama' then the likelihood is that they are referring to this alone. Without a warm-up there would be no action and without sharing there would be no re-integration into the group; both these are vital to the process, but it is the active, 'dramatic' phase which is the core of psychodrama. This enactment is seldom if ever an uncomplicated process – it tends to be multi-faceted and multi-layered. How protagonist, director and group move through this complexity is part perspiration and part inspiration. Directors draw on years of training and experience and this forms the wellspring of their spontaneity and creativity. Accurately tuning into these (which are as important to psychodrama as the spontaneity and creativity of the protagonist and auxiliaries) allows directors to make apparently inspired interventions which may not be immediately susceptible to analysis. For example, while a member of an advanced training group for practising psychodramatists facilitated by Monica Zuretti (an Argentinian psychodramatist of world renown), I and the other members of the group were often impressed by the accuracy of her insight and the quality of her interventions. With the benefit of all our years of practice, we could not always understand why she said what she said, why she did what she did. So we would ask her. With a Latin shrug, most usually she would say 'I don't know'. I found this most impressive. Monica did not need to 'know' in the sense of having reached some analytical judgement before acting. Instead, she trusted herself, the protagonist and the process, relying on her spontaneity, tele and an intuitive understanding born of practice. This made for psychodrama of high calibre.

Like most other approaches to psychotherapy and personal growth, good psychodrama relies upon these moments of inspiration as much as upon the systematic deployment of technique. Sometimes a word, a phrase or an action is just there in the forefront of the director's mind. Psychodramatists who are sufficiently rooted in theoretical understanding and grounded in practice will most often make successful and facilitative interventions if they act on these intuitive promptings even when they do not immediately understand why to say or do this is 'right'. As valuable as this inspired element is, successful psychodrama also depends upon the systematic use of techniques to give it form and structure. These techniques are the tools with which the director gives shape to the protagonist's psychodramatic journey – they are the bedrock which allows creative flights of inspiration.

Moving from Scene to Scene

In psychodrama, we have a number of aphorisms. These include, 'What the mind forgets the body often remembers', 'role reversal is the engine which drives psychodrama' and 'it takes three scenes or more to make a psychodrama'. The last is a shorthand way of indicating that, wherever and whenever the first scene of a psychodrama takes place, in a typical classical psychodrama the action is likely to move through other places and times before the denouement, that is through several scenes. Of course, protagonists are all different and each psychodrama will have its unique elements. There is no universal pattern, no recipe for a perfect psychodrama, no set number of scenes. However, the likelihood is that a familiar process will occur in most psychodramas. Perhaps most commonly, the protagonist first works with the director and the auxiliaries to enact some problem or situation in the present. This first scene will lead to some heightened awareness of the issue in another time and place, usually the past. A second scene of this past incident is established and the protagonist's exploration continues. There may be further scenes, reaching yet further into the past before a last scene in which the protagonist returns to the present with some new knowledge, increased awareness and, perhaps, resolution. It is this pattern of present – past – present which gives rise to the notion that a psychodrama must comprise at least three scenes.

Blatner (1997: 65) presents this process diagrammatically as a spiral in which the protagonist's journey is from the present, through the recent past, to the deeper past and into early childhood. The outward arm of the spiral (i.e. the return towards the present) comprises catharsis, concretization, insight and integration. Whatever the exact setting in time and space of the scenes that comprise a psychodrama, the process is always one of deepening involvement perhaps resulting in some new insight followed by a scene in which this insight is consolidated. Karp (1995: 296) refers to this as moving from the periphery of the problem to its core. This illustrates the tendency of psychodrama enactments to start on some relatively superficial level, sometimes apparently even a trivial level, before the protagonist is able to delve more deeply into the pivotal difficulty.

Blatner (1997: 72–73) is accepting of action which starts at a superficial level and offers a rationale:

> In general, people cannot tease out the essential elements in a complex welter of emotions. Layers of self-justifications and self-reproach, explanations and excuses to others, difficulty in differentiating between the actual circumstances and one's beliefs or emotional reactions to events, and similar dynamics make it impossible to develop a clear insight into the basic issues involved. Yet there is an act hunger to express and explore personally meaningful experience. Thus, it's all right to begin with some superficial event, even one which the director may feel is peripheral to more 'core' conflicts.
>
> Some therapists may see presentations of such peripheral issues as an avoidance, a kind of resistance, but in fact even these enactments can serve as a source of ideas fostering the warming-up process. Furthermore, it is an act of respect and wisdom to consider that the protagonist's unconscious may be trying to symbolically help rather than hinder. In other words, good directors go along with their protagonists rather than fight them.

Because the experience of psychodrama is real for the protagonist, the principle of always finishing action in the present is important. It might appear that a protagonist who enters a childhood scene and achieves some kind of catharsis or insight has achieved the objectives of therapy and that the drama could end. However, without a scene in which the protagonist returns to the adult state, there would be two major problems. First, the psychodramatic experience of being a child is powerful, immediate and real. In many ways, in the scene from the past, the protagonist *is* that child. It is only by following with a scene in the present that the protagonist reconnects with the adult self. Second, learning, growth and insight achieved in the psychodramatic past are only useful if they are integrated into the present. Playing out a new present scene in which the protagonist incorporates the fresh knowledge in the action is a powerful way of integrating it into the day to day being of the protagonist.

Exactly how directors and protagonists know when one scene has been played to completion varies. Sometimes the protagonist has a clearly expressed aim (for example, 'I want to meet with my father and tell him how much I miss him'), and when this has been achieved the scene has ended. Sometimes the protagonist appears to grind to a halt or in some other way prompts the director to intervene, asking if there is anything else to be done with the scene. Sometimes the protagonist appears to be in a different emotional and mental state from that in which they entered the scene. This may prompt an intervention of the type 'You look younger [or distracted, worried, helpless etc.]. I'm wondering where you are now?' Occasionally the protagonist will let the director know it is time to move on, sometimes the director's tele will provide that information and so on.

Psychodramatists facilitate their protagonist's exploration through enactment by using some or all of the techniques described in earlier chapters. Auxiliaries are encouraged to improvise around the roles they have been given, following their intuitive sense of what the person or thing they represent would have said and done. Some directors encourage spontaneous doubling by members of the audience. Amongst other techniques, mirroring and surplus reality may also have a part to play.

The Use of Role Reversal

Role reversal, the process of the protagonist playing the role of some other person or thing in the psychodrama, has two basic functions. First, it is used to show how the protagonist remembers or imagines this other person and second (and more importantly) it is a way in which the protagonist may become more aware of the situation, feelings and way of being of another. Blatner with

Blatner (1988: 174–175) refer to this as 'a way of transcending the habitual limitations of egocentricity'.

For most protagonists, their first experience of reversing roles is in the process of introducing auxiliaries into a scene. For the director to interview the protagonist in the role of another person in the scene is one of the most common ways of providing the group and the potential auxiliary with a clear picture of who this person is, what characteristics they have and how they behave. It also continues the process of the protagonist moving from the reality of the group to the reality of the unfolding psychodramatic space. Role reversal may also be used in later stages of the drama as a way of facilitating the work of the auxiliaries.

If they are uncertain how to proceed, or the protagonist indicates that they have got something wrong, the director will use role reversal to provide auxiliaries with the necessary information. The protagonist temporarily takes on the auxiliary's role and shows them and the group how that person did or would behave, saying their words in the way that the character would say them. The protagonist then reverts to their own role (which has been held by the auxiliary in the interim) and the auxiliary then repeats the words and actions they have seen and heard.

The instruction of auxiliaries is only one of the many functions of role reversal. For example, when the protagonist asks the auxiliary a question, the director may decide to let the auxiliary's spontaneity supply the answer but if the question seems particularly significant or is one to which the auxiliary cannot know the answer, then role reversal may be used. In reversed roles, the auxiliary (as the protagonist) asks the question of the protagonist (in the auxiliary role) who replies. The two then 'reverse back' (that is take once more their own roles in the enactment) and the protagonist asks the question again. This time the auxiliary supplies the answer heard in the protagonist's role.

One of the many apparently 'magical' elements of psychodrama is that in the role of the other, the protagonist will often know the answer to the question whereas as themselves they seemingly do not. Hearing this answer in their own role can be a powerful experience. The answering of questions can be seen as a special case of the instruction of auxiliaries but it is much more than that. What is important, what supplies the answer, is that the protagonist experiences the world as the other person and sees it from that person's frame of reference.

Kellerman (1992: 148) discusses the value of allowing protagonists to take and hold the role of another for a longer time than would be necessary to instruct an auxiliary or to answer a question. This can often allow insight which is denied to the protagonist in their own role and/or the expression of feelings which are otherwise inaccessible to the protagonist. For example, a protagonist who has been so browbeaten and bullied as to become naturally appeasing, unassertive and deferential may be so deeply unconsciously in control of angry or aggressive feelings that, in their own persona, they simply do not emerge into consciousness let alone be expressed. Playing the role of an angry or aggressive person (perhaps the abuser, but if this seems too daunting then someone else) may very well allow a real connection with and expression of the protagonist's own anger.

Generally speaking, when role reversal is used as a way of allowing insight into the world of another, it is because the director perceives some value in the protagonist empathizing with the other person. In reversed roles, the protagonist has the experience of seeing the world through the eyes of another and of seeing themselves as another sees them. Both of these elements of role reversal are of great significance in the development of what Kellerman (1992: 85–95) refers to as 'action insight'. He states (p. 86):

> Action insight is the result of various kinds of action learning. It may be defined as the integration of emotional, cognitive, imaginary, behavioural and interpersonal learning experiences. . . . [It] cannot be attained through introspective analysis while lying on the couch. It is achieved only in action, while moving about, standing still, pushing and pulling, making sounds or gestures or pronouncing words.

and (pp. 90–91):

> The first and most obvious characteristic of action insight is that it is based on an actual personal learning experience and not merely verbal information. . . . For example, it would be meaningless to tell an overprotective mother to be less protective. However if, in psychodrama, she is persuaded to reverse roles with her child, even for a short time, and to experience intensely how it feels to live under her own protective behaviour, she might change. Such a first-hand awareness may give the protagonist an experience which is sufficiently meaningful to produce a lasting impact.

Through action and, in this instance, specifically through role reversal, learning and insight are embodied.

Doubling

The two types of doubling may each have a part to play as an enactment progresses. Both depend upon the empathic skills of the person doing the doubling for their success. The task of a double is to see the world through the eyes of the protagonist and to act or speak from their understanding of it – that is, as if they were the protagonist. Successful doubles set aside their own perceptual frameworks and their interventions represent the views and thoughts of the protagonist not their own. Mimicking body language often provides a kinaesthetic sense of what it is like to be another, how they are feeling, and this is valuable to doubles.

Directors may offer protagonists a permanent double when they sense that the scene or situation is particularly challenging or inhibiting for the protagonist. The permanent double forms an alliance with the protagonist. This is of itself a support and there is an explicit understanding that, should the protagonist find some action too difficult to perform, the double will act or speak for them. Frequently the double's intervention facilitates the protagonist to express themselves in their own way and often the presence of the double is enabling of itself.

Spontaneous doubling, the technique which allows members of the audience (and sometimes the director) to speak for the protagonist when they sense that something is being unsaid or unexpressed, may also be helpful as a psychodrama develops. Some psychodramatists encourage it as a way of facilitating action, for others, this process is of limited value. For those who take the first position, spontaneous doubling is a way of increasing the involvement of the audience in the drama and of making use of the wisdom of the group. They see it as a helpful way of intervening when a protagonist is stuck or cannot say for themselves what in their heart and soul they wish to say. Allowing a spontaneous double may break this deadlock. It is also an important demonstration of the involvement of the group with the protagonist. The second position is that it is the protagonist's perception and experience which is important and that 'stuckness' may be an essential part of the process, with which doubling would interfere. For directors who take this view, role reversal is seen as much more likely to be helpful.

ACTION

Mirroring

A protagonist can be in the position of being 'unable to see the wood for the trees', that is, so closely involved in the drama as to be unable to form a critical judgement of their own actions or those of others. This might be especially true when the scene is highly charged emotionally or involves some young or easily dominated aspect of the protagonist, that is, a role in which the mature, adult judgement of the protagonist is somehow in abeyance. When this appears to be happening, the director may invite the protagonist to step outside the scene and to watch as another member of the group takes the protagonist's part. This is the technique of mirroring, which Blatner with Blatner (1988: 169) refer to as the 'human version of videotape playback'. Directors may also use mirroring when protagonists seem blind to the effects of their behaviour on others. It offers instant feedback, protagonists get the opportunity to see themselves as others see them and to witness the effects they have from a more objective perspective.

Surplus Reality

Surplus reality has a role in the progress of a psychodrama when a need to enact something which did not happen, can never happen or will never happen emerges. This may be about 'unfinished business', for example saying farewell to a dead relative, or it may be an opportunity to replay a life event in such a way as to give the protagonist the opportunity to behave differently. This may be experimentation ('What would happen if I did it this way?') or a chance to experience something which did not happen but which might be beneficial, for example good parenting from a tender, loving and respectful mother for a protagonist from an abusive background.

A Psychodrama

DETERMINING THE ISSUE, SETTING THE SCENE AND FINDING THE AUXILIARIES
With the support of the group, Virginia was to be protagonist. She was a bit vague about where her psychodrama might

93

*start. Perhaps it was something to do with her computer,
perhaps it was about her kitchen. David, the director, asked
her if these two things had something in common. 'Yes!'
asserted Virginia. 'I can't get away from either of them. They
dominate my life. I hadn't realized that until you asked. I'm
always at somebody else's beck and call. At work that evil one-
eyed monster keeps me at it all the time, at home I'm always
in the kitchen cooking, washing up, doing the washing,
making packed lunches for the kids. I'm even thinking of
moving my bed in there!'*

*'So is there something about never having time to your-
self?' questioned David. 'Would a good place to start be at
work or in your kitchen?'*

*Virginia decided that it was in her kitchen that she felt
herself to have least freedom and she decided to show the
group what it was like to be her just before a family meal
time.*

*Virginia chose to re-enact the events of a hectic tea-time
from just a few days before. She worked with David to
establish the scene, using chairs and tables to represent the
cooker, the sink, the washing machine and the cupboards.*

'Who else is in the kitchen?' asked David.

*'Zoe, my daughter is washing her hands at the sink – the
boys are in the sitting room. I can't see them but I can hear
them. As usual, they are screaming and shouting at each other
and they've got the television on too loud,' said Virginia.*

*'I guess we need to find someone to play Zoe – what about
the boys?' asked David.*

SCENE 1: THE PRESENT

*Virginia found auxiliaries for Zoe and her two sons, Ben and
Dominic, and the action began. The scene had been playing
for a few minutes, the boys were increasingly noisy, ignoring Virginia's demand that they stop fighting, Zoe kept asking questions and in other ways pestering her mother and
Virginia was becoming increasingly shrill as she tried to
cope with burning fishfingers and fractious children. In the
midst of all this, Virginia went suddenly silent.*

*Hannah indicated to David that she would like to double
for Virginia. Virginia assented. Standing behind Virginia
and placing a hand on her shoulder Hannah said, 'I wish
they would all go away – I wish everyone would go away and*

*just leave me alone.' And then, raising her voice, 'You are
nasty whinging brats and I hate you! Just piss off and leave
me alone!'*

'Is that right?' David asked Virginia.

*'Some of it – I don't hate them . . . but I do wish they'd just
go away. I just want a bit of peace. Is that too much to
ask?'*

*'Can you say that to them in your own words?' enquired
David.*

*Looking directly at her children, Virginia shouted, 'Just
shut up all of you – I've had enough. Just go away – leave me
alone.' Then she whispered, 'If you won't leave me, then I'll
leave you.' Virginia looked stunned and ashamed by her
words.*

*David invited Virginia to step outside her scene. 'If you
won't leave me then I'll leave you,' he repeated. 'That seemed
important – I'm wondering if it was familiar in some
way?'*

*'That's exactly what the children's father said to me as he
left us – I'd almost forgotten. It was an awful night. He just
went and we haven't really spoken since,' said Virginia.*

'Can you show us what happened?' asked David.

SCENE 2: THE NEAR PAST

*Virginia dismantled her first scene and, with David's help,
reconstructed the sitting room of the house in which she had
lived with her children and Gerry, her ex-husband. She chose
Hannah to play the part of Gerry and their final row was re-
enacted. As Hannah/Gerry flung the words 'If you won't leave
me then I'll leave you' at her and stormed out of the room and
the house, Virginia appeared to collapse into herself. She
looked very sad, lost and abandoned. She was very still and
quiet. Eventually David gently approached her and asked if
he could double for her. Virginia nodded almost impercepti-
bly.*

*'I'm so lost and alone – nobody cares about me – if life is
like this then I don't want to live,' David paused. 'Is that right
Virginia?' Virginia's reply was a series of deep, gut-
wrenching sobs dissolving into floods of tears. The group was
quietly attentive as David looked round at them, he saw that
while several members of the audience were obviously deeply
moved, they were being cared for by others.*

95

Soon, Virginia looked up. 'My mum did that to me too,' she whispered.

'Your mum did that?' echoed David.

'Yes – when I was four she walked out on me – left me. I was only four. How could she do that?'

'Is that a place to go from here?' asked David.

'I don't really want to but I guess I've got to haven't I?' said Virginia.

'It's your psychodrama – we can do whatever you want,' said David.

'OK – but can I stop if I can't take it?' Virginia asked.

'Of course you can – but I guess what you are telling us is that to go back to that time when your mother walked out on you is going to be difficult. I wonder if you would like to have a double? Someone to be with and support you, speak for you when it's too difficult?' asked David.

'No – I don't think so. I want to do this on my own,' Virginia said firmly.

SCENE 3: THE DISTANT PAST

The scene was set in the big farmhouse kitchen in the house in which Virginia had lived as a child. It had a wooden floor, a scrubbed pine table which could easily seat ten, an old-fashioned deep, square sink, a few rag rugs, metal hooks in the ceiling, a large Aga cooker and an assortment of hard and soft chairs. Coats hung on hooks on the door to the outside, and shoes and Wellington boots of various sizes stood against the nearby wall. Virginia's recall of this kitchen was so vivid that David and other members of the group could almost see it appearing before their eyes.

Virginia was sure that the scene took place in the early afternoon. Her brothers were at school and her father at work. She was playing with her favourite doll on the kitchen floor while her mother (played by Deena and called Mummy by the young Virginia) was busy with her chores. Virginia was so absorbed in her play that she wasn't really aware of her mother bustling about the kitchen as she absently got under her feet. Mummy tripped and fell, breaking the pots she was carrying. As she rose to her feet, she began to scream insanely at Virginia, calling her a stupid little bitch.

David noticed that Virginia looked a little unsure and he stopped the action. 'Is this right?' he asked.

'Almost – but she was much more vicious and violent. She broke my doll,' said Virginia.

'OK – reverse roles and be your mum,' said David.

As Mummy, Virginia shouted and screamed, pushing and shoving little Virginia all over the kitchen. 'I can't stand you, you little bitch. I never wanted you. You're nothing but a nuisance.' Tears of rage poured down Virginia's cheeks as she picked up the teddy bear which was playing the part of her favourite doll. 'This is what I'd like to do to you,' she screamed as she swung it by its feet, hitting it repeatedly against the Aga. 'That's it – I've had enough. I'm going,' she said, slamming the doll down onto the floor and storming out through the back door.

'Reverse back,' said David. 'OK, Deena, let's have as much of that as you can remember.' The scene was replayed with Virginia in her role as her four-year-old self.

As Mummy stormed out of the kitchen, Virginia collapsed on the floor, her head buried in her arms. David carefully approached her and put his hand on her shoulder. 'Your Mummy's gone,' he said kindly, 'You look very lost and alone – and so very unhappy, bewildered and battered. Can you tell us what you are thinking and feeling?'

'I've been bad again. I'm so bad, Mummy's gone. She said she would and it's all my fault,' sobbed Virginia. 'Nobody likes me – they all think I'm bad. They don't want me.'

'You are only four,' said David. 'Your Mummy has just left you and you think it is your fault and that everybody hates you. As I kneel next to you, I can feel that you are ashamed. When you are ready, I'd like you to look around the group and tell me what you see.'

'I can't do that – they think I'm silly,' murmured Virginia.

'That isn't what I see as I look around,' said David. 'Risk a quick peep.'

Virginia looked around at the other members of the group. She saw tender smiles, tear-stained faces, compassion and understanding everywhere. She grew noticeably stronger, unfolding herself and sitting upright.

SCENE 4: MIRRORING

'Virginia,' said David, 'I'd really like you to have the opportunity to see this scene with your mother as we saw it. Would

97

you please come out of the kitchen and pick someone to be the four-year-old you?'

Virginia was initially reluctant to cast somebody as herself. She said it was too awful an experience, but she did finally pick Gareth to play her part and she witnessed the scene from the outside. As Mummy left the kitchen, Virginia turned to David and said in a surprised tone, 'It wasn't my fault at all was it? She was totally over the top. I was just playing.' And more angrily, 'What a wicked thing to do, smash poor Joanna like that. I loved that doll. I still do – there has never been another like her.'

There were a few moments of silence and then Virginia said, 'But why? Why did she do that? Why did she go? I didn't know that she would come back. And she did that sort of thing many times. Was she crazy or what? How could she do that to me? I was only four!'

SCENES 5 AND 6: TWO SCENES IN SURPLUS REALITY
'You're asking why,' said David. 'Who do you think knows?'
'She does,' spat Virginia in the direction of Mummy.
'Do you want to ask her?' enquired David.

Virginia decided that she would like to ask her mother just what was going on that afternoon and on the similar, later, occasions she now remembered. She said too that she wanted the opportunity to tell her mother how abandoned she had felt then and, in a way, ever since. Together, Virginia and David decided that it would be better if the meeting with Virginia's mother happened in a place and time of Virginia's choosing. It would be the adult Virginia who questioned Mummy, not the vulnerable four-year-old. The scene was established and Deena continued her role.

'Why were you such a heartless bitch?' demanded Virginia of Mummy. 'What was wrong with me? How could you treat a little four-year-old like that?'

'Reverse roles,' said David and the question was repeated to Virginia in Mummy's role.

As her mother, Virginia at first denied any ill-treatment of her daughter, saying that she never meant any harm. David made use of role reversal to allow adult Virginia to interrogate Mummy and to answer from that role. What emerged was a tale of a woman on the verge of madness. She had thought her family complete when the last of her two sons was born and then, ten years later, an unplanned and unwanted little girl came along. By this time, the relationship between Mummy and Virginia's father had deteriorated, Virginia's birth strained it to breaking point, each of her parents blaming the other and resentful of the baby. Virginia's parents now scarcely spoke and Mummy saw herself as little more than a servant charged with caring for her husband, her children and the house. She longed to escape and to live a life of her own.

After this disclosure, Virginia in her own role, told Mummy just how awful it had been for her as a four-year-old. In her final expression of anger to Mummy she shouted, 'OK life was rotten for you – I can see that, but I was only four years old. Whatever was happening for you it wasn't my fault. I was blameless and you made my life hell. I was a little girl – scarcely more than a baby really – you were the adult. You should have cared for me and made me safe!'

When it was clear that the scene was over, David asked Virginia who could offer the comfort and care which had been missing in her early life. 'I could now,' she replied. David offered her the chance for a short scene in which she, the adult Virginia, met with her four-year-old self. The meeting took place away from the house in which so many horrors had happened. Virginia cradled Gareth as her four-year-old self in her arms and said, 'Mummy was crazy you know. It wasn't you that was bad. You are a beautiful little girl and it isn't true that nobody wants you. I want you. I love you and need you.'

David asked Virginia and Gareth to reverse roles and, now as older Virginia, Gareth repeated the words he had heard. Tears moistened the eyes of the two players and many of the audience. A sense of deep peace and calm came over everybody as Gareth held Virginia and rocked her gently, saying 'You are beautiful. You are good. You are wanted.'

David allowed this peaceful scene between Gareth and Virginia to go on for a while before, aware of the fast approaching end of the session, he approached them and asked them to reverse roles. To the once-again adult Virginia, he said, 'We're getting close to the end of the session and I'd like you to have a scene in which you return to the present and we must allow time for sharing too. Before we do all that, *is there anything else you want to say to your four-year-old self?'*

'No, I don't think so – she knows I am always here for her now – she wasn't sure before.'

SCENE 7: RETURN TO THE PRESENT

In her last scene, Virginia returned to the setting of the first scene and met once more with her children. She told them how much she loved them and that she was very sorry for wishing that they would go away. She hugged them and listened with enthusiasm to the tales they told of their days at school. The scene finished with a promise of bedtime stories for all and expressions of warmth and happiness on the faces of Virginia and the auxiliaries.

'Right,' said David, as Virginia dismantled the scene and the auxiliaries returned to their seats. Now some sharing.'

Virginia's psychodrama, like all others, is unique but it does exemplify not only the way in which enaction moves from scene to scene and how some of the techniques of psychodrama may be employed, but also some of its effects. On her inward spiral, Virginia moved from her rejection of others (her own children), through a recent experience of being rejected and abandoned to an earlier (perhaps even primal) similar experience. This journey involved a heightening of emotion and vulnerability. On her outward spiral, Virginia achieved some emotional insight in the mirroring scene which was consolidated in the second scene in surplus reality. The two surplus reality scenes also contained elements of catharsis. In the first, Virginia was able to contact and express some of her angry feelings towards her mother, the second allowed an upwelling of love and tenderness towards herself and towards others. This was an emotional release which had been long denied. The last scene allowed Virginia to bring her emotional insight into the present and to express love towards her own children. This can be viewed as a considerable movement towards resolution.

7

THE THIRD SCENE: COMPLETING THE SESSION

When the last scene of an enactment is completed, the auxiliaries and the protagonist return to their places in the group. Some directors invite the protagonist to sit beside them during the last phase of psychodrama (known as sharing). This is a symbolic continuation of the intimate relationship between director and protagonist and allows the protagonist to feel supported throughout the re-integration offered through the sharing process. In sharing, the focus begins to shift from the protagonist towards the audience. The protagonist is still the major figure but other members of the group now have a chance to give expression to some of their own thoughts and feelings as they relate to the enactment and the protagonist.

The Role of the Audience

The audience is an important element of psychodrama. It is an aid to the protagonist, while its members are also helped by the enactment. It serves as a pool from which auxiliaries may be drawn and as a source of spontaneous doubling, but those members of the group who witness the action without playing any other part are also serving a vital function. In their enactment, protagonists are 'telling' a story of their lives, showing what it is like to be them. Jan Costa (personal communication, 1993) likens this to the process of giving testimony. Because this story has the immediacy of re-enactment as if it were the present, it is a more powerful testimony than that given in words could ever be. In a very real sense, the protagonist is reliving the events and inviting the group to witness them. As attentive and active witnesses to this testimony, the director and the audience can make real connections with the world of the protagonist and tacitly offer acceptance, encouragement and support. For the protagonist, this witnessing can of itself be therapeutic – being acceptingly seen, heard and understood is a first step to healing.

These qualities of acceptance (or unconditional positive regard) and empathy are cornerstones of the person-centred approach (see, for example, Mearns and Thorne, 1988), and Rogers (1957: 96) wrote of how they (amongst others) were essential attributes of the therapist in *any* successful psychotherapy. One of the strengths of psychodrama is that the protagonist can receive empathy and acceptance not only from the director but also from the audience (see Wilkins, 1994a: 17): this greatly increases their efficacy. The acceptance and empathy of the audience do not necessarily come automatically but are likely to be products of group process. The expression and exploration of personally meaningful material is directly dependent upon the establishment of a climate of trust which itself depends upon the ability of the group to accept the expression of negative feelings (classically as an attack on the group leader). In group process terms (see Corey, 1994: 279–280), expression of personal material (giving testimony) is responded to by the development of a healing capacity within the group (the expression of empathy and acceptance). This is integral to the power of psychodrama and can be promoted by directors through attention to group process.

There is a great temptation to see psychodrama as protagonist-centred. It is the protagonist's issue which is being addressed through enactment, and it is they who achieve catharsis, insight and/or resolution. Perhaps by taking the chance in role to express some part of themselves otherwise suppressed or denied, the auxiliaries benefit too, but even so this seems peripheral to the apparent main purpose, which is for the director to work with the protagonist to the benefit of the latter. To take this view loses sight of the fact that psychodrama is (most commonly) a group approach. Those members of a psychodrama group not involved in the action can be as intimately involved in their own psychotherapeutic processes as protagonists are in theirs. For the most part, this happens when members of the audience identify with the protagonist (or perhaps one of the auxiliaries) and the emotions they see revealed in the enactment resonate with or awaken feelings of their own. This can lead to a catharsis which echoes that of the protagonist – Karp (1995: 296) refers to the way in which watching the enactment of another's life story can purge the audience member and likens this to Greek drama. Sometimes the effect is, for example, to arouse, lend immediacy to or bring to consciousness an unresolved issue. This can be a spur to further work, perhaps as protagonist at a later time, or the group member may choose to speak in the sharing portion of the psychodrama session which may bring about some relief or resolution. Casson (1997a: 43–54) has written at some length of the therapeutic effects of being in the audience in a variety of dramatic settings, including psychodrama.

Although the engagement of the audience in any psychodrama is continuous, it is the third element, sharing, in which they are most actively involved.

Sharing

As the last scene in any psychodrama enactment closes, the director will invite sharing from the audience. This is an activity in which the protagonist hears from any and all the group members who wish to speak about their involvement in the psychodrama: the protagonist merely listens. Sharing is of two types, each with several functions. First, there is sharing from role. Every person who has been an auxiliary in the enactment, however briefly, is invited to tell the protagonist what it was like to be in that role. This is an opportunity for the auxiliaries to 'de-role', that is to lose the attributes and characteristics they temporarily adopted and to reclaim their own. Sometimes this is done almost ritually, especially if the role has been difficult or auxiliaries find it hard to free themselves. This example is from Virginia's psychodrama described in Chapter 6:

> David had invited sharing from role and Deena spoke first. Looking at Virginia, she said, 'As Mummy I felt really hateful towards little Virginia. I just couldn't stand to have you anywhere near me and I really wanted to hurt you – make you feel like I was feeling. Deep inside I knew it wasn't your fault but I really resented you for existing at all. But I'm not Mummy, I'm Deena – I'm a good mother – I love my children and never smack them.'

'Is that enough?' asked David. 'Are you rid of Mummy?'
'I'm not sure,' replied Deena. 'I think she is still hanging around somewhere and I'd like to shake her off!'
'Do that then,' said David. 'Stand up and give yourself a good shake, telling yourself and us that you are getting her out of your system.'
Deena stood up, shook herself and brushed herself down with her hands saying: 'I'm not Virginia's Mummy, I'm Deena.'
'Better?' asked David.
'Much,' replied Deena.
'OK then – let's have some more sharing,' David said.

The second function of sharing from role is to provide the protagonist with more information. Often, auxiliaries do not have the chance to express everything they experience in role. Sometimes this is to do with the characteristics of the person they are portraying, sometimes they have not been asked the right questions or been given the appropriate prompts. Telling the protagonist of what has been experienced but not expressed can be helpful to both – the auxiliary discharges the unexpressed thoughts or feelings, the protagonist can gain further insight.

Karen's psychodrama had included a scene in which she confronted her boss, who had been played by Steve. In the scene, Karen had been assertive, expressing her sense of frustration, but had been unable to get any more response from Steve than a stony stare and an instruction to calm down and go through proper channels. In sharing, Steve said, 'As your boss, Karen, I felt really intimidated at first but as you calmly persisted, I began to admire you. I still didn't know how to respond to you but I ended up really listening to what you had to say. At first I thought, "Here's another silly woman" but that changed. I couldn't let you see it, but you made quite an impression on me. I'll probably do what you asked.'

After sharing from role, group members are asked to share personally with the protagonist. That is, to tell of what in their own lives is similar to aspects of the protagonist's story. Kellerman (1992: 161) writes: 'Sharing, with its focus on universality and existential validation, encourages identification with the protagonist in a personal, emotionally involved manner.' This type of sharing is not an opportunity for analysis and still less, criticism. Karp (1995: 296) states:

> Sharing is a time for group catharsis and integration. It was meant as a 'love-back' rather than feedback, discouraging analysis of the event and encouraging identifications. Points of involvement by individual group members are identified, and each member finds out how he or she is like the protagonist.

At the end of their enactments, protagonists can feel exposed and vulnerable. They have in effect revealed themselves much more than if they had spoken of the feelings and events enacted and may be unsure as to how their story has been received. In receiving sharing from the auxiliaries, the audience and, in some schools of psychodrama, the director, the protagonist hears people saying 'I am like you in this way'. This process reconnects the protagonist with the rest of the group. More subtly, as group members share with the protagonist, it is likely that they are also communicating their acceptance and empathy, the therapeutic benefits of which are outlined above.

Although it is often presented as primarily of benefit to the protagonist, sharing also plays an important part in the development and healing of other group members. To those who watch or who are auxiliaries, psychodrama can be evocative, provocative and stimulating. Strong feelings may be aroused, painful memories awakened. Sharing is an opportunity to give at least limited expression to these feelings and memories. This has the double effect of re-including the protagonist in the group and relieving the group member. Unexpressed feelings can lead to a range of psychological and physiological symptoms, ranging from the unpleasant or inconvenient to the distressing. My advice to members of my psychodrama groups is to at least openly name these feelings or risk going home with a headache!

Some examples of sharing after Virginia's psychodrama in Chapter 6 may help to illustrate its effects and benefits.

After all the auxiliaries had said something about their experiences in role, David invited personal sharing from the group. Michelle was first to speak to Virginia.

'I couldn't believe it when you did your first scene – that could have been me. Sometimes, being a single mum is just too much and I just want to get away and have a life of my

own. I can't stand my kids sometimes but I know I love them really.

'When you met yours again in the last scene, I felt really tearful. All that love really got to me – I liked it and I guess I was feeling my love for my kids – but also how much I miss my Mum. I want someone to love me like that.'

Deena shared next. 'I knew you were going to pick me to play your Mummy. She's just like my mum. What happened between us was different but I never felt loved or wanted by her and she would say and do some really crazy things. She used to hit me and sometimes I didn't know why. Sometimes I knew what I had done that was naughty but sometimes I'd just got smacked for no particular reason. Well, I guess there was a reason, but it had more to do with her than me.' Deena paused and she looked deeply sorrowful. 'The crazy thing is I miss her and I still want her in my life even though she has gone now.'

As Deena began to cry softly, Gareth put his arm around her and said to Virginia, 'I was really glad to be little Virginia. To receive all that warmth and loving from you gave me the strength to look at my own failure as a dad. And then when I got to reverse roles and to show you warmth and love, I was so pleased to really feel like that. I felt it towards you but I was also talking to my daughter. I haven't seen her now for ages and I know I made a mess of being her dad. But I do love her and I miss her.'

David chose to share next. 'It takes me a while after I have directed to become aware of my own connections with the work. I was really with you Virginia as we worked together and didn't really have time to think about myself, but as I sit here now, all sorts of similarities are striking me. I think I most want to tell you about my teddy bear. His name was Clarence – I don't know why, it just was – and I had him from being a baby. I don't remember a time before Clarence. We went everywhere together and he was my best friend. Anyway, to cut a long story short, I came home from school one day to find that he had gone from the chair in my bedroom where he lived – I was about eleven and didn't take him to bed with me any more. I asked my mum where he was and she told me that she had thrown him away. I couldn't believe it – how could she do that? What right did she have?

He was a person and he was mine. I still haven't forgiven her and as I'm telling you this I feel a mixture of rage and deep, deep loss.'

There were a few moments of silence before Gerry spoke, his voice shaky and his manner subdued. 'I could hardly bear it when you did that scene with your Gerry. I remember how I broke up with my partner. It was awful. I think we both knew that things couldn't go on the way they were but I really was a pig. In the end, I just upped and went. She wanted to talk about it but I just couldn't stand to go through all that all over again. It was right to part but I do so wish I'd done it differently – we'd done it differently.'

Other members of the group shared about their children, about their parents and about how difficult it had sometimes been as a child to separate themselves from their parents' behaviour. As young children, most of the group had some experience of seeing themselves as causes of their parents' anger or distress when this wasn't so. Other group members spoke of the experience of being deserted or abandoned – and a few, with some personal difficulty, of deserting others. Everybody spoke to Virginia and the sharing was on a very deep level. As the sharing came to an end, the atmosphere in the group room was intensely calm, people were sitting closer to one another, some had arms round others, some were lost deep in their own thoughts but it was as if the group as a whole was at peace with itself.

Closure

As with any other approach to psychotherapy, endings are important in psychodrama. Psychodramas end, individual sessions end and psychodrama groups usually have a finite life – even those that do not will see members leave as they achieve their aims or move on for some other reason. All of these endings must be managed and facilitated and, although the group may share it, this is principally the responsibility of the group leader. As well as practical issues (for example those related to time), there are psychotherapeutic considerations to these endings. Ideally, good therapy culminates in integration; certainly there is an implication that the process will in some way be complete. The process of achieving this completion is often referred to as 'closure', although, as Kellerman (1992: 152–153) points out, this was not originally a psychodramatic concept.

In psychodrama, closure may refer to the end of an individual psychodrama, its grand finale, the scene in which the protagonist's learning is consolidated. It may also refer to the intrapsychic process of the protagonist. Kellerman (1992: 153) writes:

> From the point of view of psychotherapy, closure is a kind of intra-psychic conclusion for the protagonist. As such, it represents the maturation of a healing process, the final station of a therapeutic journey, and the goal of a session, ideally giving a feeling of emotional relief and a sense of therapeutic progress. It is in this termination phase of psychodrama psychotherapy that the definitive work of resolution is anchored.

It would be mistaken to believe that closure of this kind always happens in the last scene of a psychodrama or even in sharing. Psychotherapy and personal growth are processes; that is, they are characterized by change over time. A psychodrama session may be cathartic and lead to insight but it rarely results in an instantaneous and permanent change. More likely is that the learning from psychodrama is gradually consolidated in the protagonist's life outside the group. In this sense, closure too is a process; however, psychodrama directors do have a responsibility to ensure that protagonists end their enactments in an integrated and adult state (by, for example, finishing the action in the present) and that they are re-included in the group through adequate sharing: this constitutes closure of a kind.

Seeking closure is not necessarily the same as seeking a happy ending. Kellerman (1992: 156–157) asserts that there is a 'major controversy' about the introduction of happy endings to psychodrama. On the one hand, optimistic endings are seen as positive reinforcement and as aesthetically pleasing; on the other they are seen as distorting reality and thus counter-therapeutic. I take the view that to introduce anything from the perspective of the director (or the director's understanding of the desires of the group) is unlikely to help the protagonist. If the protagonist is in reality stuck, uncertain or in conflict then perhaps for the director and the group to recognize and accept this is important. No useful purpose will be served by imposing a fairy-tale ending.

Ideally, a scene in which the protagonist achieves closure of the desired kind emerges naturally and at their instigation or by negotiation with the director. When this does not happen, a number of solutions are available. As a person-centred psycho-dramatist, I am likely to turn my attention to the process between myself and the protagonist on the assumption that it mirrors or echoes the difficulty the protagonist is experiencing. Directly addressing this may ease the log jam. An alternative is for directors to suggest a closing scene drawing on their experience and what has gone before in the enactment. Kellerman (1992: 157–159) categorizes 'common closure scenes' and lists twenty-nine types. He (1992: 153) also points out that closure is likewise important for auxiliaries, the audience and the director. Sharing from role and formal de-roling offer auxiliaries closure and the audience has its opportunity for closure by acknowledging feelings and connections in sharing. Directors may also achieve closure in sharing but, for them, debriefing with a co-therapist or in supervision may also be part of this process.

Closing sessions is important too. The post-enactment sharing may be sufficient for a group to achieve closure but often some further interaction which involves the whole group is helpful. Blatner (1997: 107–108) refers to 'some components of closing' which may 'lead to a further winding down of the level of tension'. These include:

- Planning the next session.
- Supporting vulnerable or distressed group members (by, for example, offering positive feedback).
- Addressing unfinished business between group members.
- Closing rituals (for example, simply holding hands in a circle).

In my own sessions, I am usually less structured. I turn my attention from the protagonist to the group as a whole – that is, I cease to be a director and reassume the role of group facilitator. I acknowledge the impact the psychodrama has had on individuals and respond to the present feelings of which I am aware. I also encourage interaction between group members. My invitation is most often, 'Is there anything anyone would like to say or ask?' Responses to this vary, but it does open the door to unfinished business.

The end of the lifetime of a psychodrama group presents the need for closure of yet another kind. In my view, the last session of a psychodrama group is as important as the first (see Chapter 4). It is the last opportunity for group members to say what has so far been unsaid and to do the things they wished they had done. It is also a time to celebrate the existence of the group and to begin the process of mourning its passing. How psychodramatists do this varies greatly but the issues to be addressed are always similar.

It may be important to allow any group members who have not been a protagonist or whose work is in some way unfinished the chance to address this. Some directors will set aside part of the last session for vignettes in which group members can at least raise their unaddressed material. This is an opportunity to be heard in the group (which can itself be beneficial) and it can be a way of flagging up remaining psychotherapeutic needs or giving a commitment to future work. For example:

It was the last session of the psychodrama group. Its members had been together through tears, laughter, anger and regret for ten weeks now. The enactments had been intensely involving but not everybody had taken the opportunity to be protagonist. Keith was one of these group members, although he had been an auxiliary several times. Terry, the group leader, moved two chairs into the centre of the group and put them about two metres apart, facing each other. He said, 'This evening is your last opportunity to show us something from your own lives. We haven't got much time because there are lots of other things we need to do but we can do three or four ten minute vignettes. This is a chance to do a brief piece of work, say something you haven't said – or perhaps it is about identifying work to do in the future – making some kind of commitment to yourself. Just come and take one of the seats and tell us who is on the other and what the vignette will be about.' Terry turned and looked round the group, 'Anyone up for it?' he asked.

Keith stepped forward. 'On that chair,' he said pointing, 'is my dad. I just want to tell him how much I miss him.'

'OK,' said Terry, 'See your dad sitting on the other chair and tell him what you want him to hear.'

'Hello, Dad,' said Keith. 'I've been avoiding you for ten weeks – well I suppose I've been avoiding you ever since you died – but I can't go home tonight without saying something to you.' There was a long pause, then Keith whispered, 'But now you are here, I don't know what to say.'

Ruth indicated to Terry that she would like to double for Keith and Terry nodded. Standing behind Keith's chair with her right hand on his left shoulder, Ruth said, 'Dad, I really miss you. I know we never said much to each other but now you've gone I really hurt and I don't know how to tell anyone, how to show my pain.'

Looking at his dad's chair, Keith said, 'Yeah – that's right. I do miss you, I do hurt and I can't show it. I can't talk about it. You always told me men don't cry – that's women's work. I'm not sure you were right about that. I guess there are lots of things I have to sort out about you – maybe next time.'

'Maybe next time,' repeated Terry. 'Is there anything else you want to say to your dad while he is here?'

'No – only I love you. I do wish I could have said that to you while you were alive. And I wish you had said it to me,' sighed Keith.

Vignettes are one way of offering individuals the opportunity for closure but there is also a need for the group to find a way of closing. This can be done in a variety of ways but perhaps the most widely used techniques and exercises are those which allow group members to give some expression to their attachment to the group, what they have gained from being a part of it, what they will take away (and perhaps what they will leave behind) and to offer each other feedback. In my own practice, I echo the exercises I used in the first group session. For example, if I used a chair or cushion to represent the group and asked people to arrange themselves in relation to it and then make a personal statement about the group, I use the same chair in the last session. This time the invitation is for group members to again place themselves in relation to the chair as representing the group, to notice how that is different (if it is) from where they originally put themselves, and to say something about their feelings. Almost invariably, group members are closer to each other and to whatever it is that represents the group and most people speak of warmth and closeness. There are other exercises I might use:

The group was half-way through its last session. Paul put a pile of large sheets of paper and a box of felt-tip pens in the centre of the room. 'Right,' he said, 'This is an opportunity for each of us to offer the others some positive feedback and to have something concrete to take away with us. What I'd like each of us to do is to take a sheet of paper, write our names on the top and then leave it somewhere on the floor. When we have done that, the task is to write as little or as much as you want – within reason – on everybody else's sheet. The idea I have is that this is something we have appreciated about that person in this group. There may be other things you want to do as well.'

There was a flurry of activity as the group members set about the task. Apart from the occasional cry of 'Who's got Jane – I haven't done her yet' or something similar, the group was absorbed in this task for over twenty minutes. Paul looked around and it seemed to him that everybody had finished. 'Is everybody done?' he asked. 'Yes? OK then find your own sheet and read what people have said about you then we'll get together for some sharing about that before we do the last exercise.'

When they had read their sheets, the group came together in a circle and took the opportunity to say what they felt about the feedback they had received. These were moments of great tenderness and warmth. Eventually, Paul said, 'OK, these are our last few minutes together. We've all had the opportunity to say things to each other and about the group but I wonder if there is anything else anyone wants to say or ask before we finish?' Nobody spoke. 'OK,' said Paul, 'let's stand up, push the chairs out of the way and stand together in a circle.' When this was done, Paul said, 'Now we are going to say goodbye to ourselves as this group but I'd like to do that in a ceremonial way.

'Take the hands of the people on either side and look around the group, making eye-contact if you can.

'Now each of us is going to have the opportunity to name one thing we are leaving behind in this room and one thing we are taking away. Then we will all take one pace backwards and say goodbye, then another pace backwards and drop our hands. And that will be it.'

Irene spoke first, 'I'm leaving behind some of the anger I have for my sister – and I am taking away the love and support I have felt from you all.'

'I'm leaving behind my shyness,' said Dennis, 'and I'm taking away the knowledge that my views are as valid as anyone else's.'

Looking round at everyone, Jamie said sadly, 'I'm leaving some anger, some sorrow but I am taking away so much that I don't know where to start. I guess I feel cherished here and I'm taking some of that away with me.'

When everyone had spoken, they took the two paces back and the session and the group came to an end.

Kellerman (1992: 160) encapsulates almost poetically the purpose and impact of closure in psychodrama thus:

> In the final analysis, the ultimate purpose of closure in psychodrama is to extend the drama beyond its natural end and induce a transition to a new beginning. At the cross-roads of closure, the protagonist reflects upon what happened in the past, recognises what exists in the present and looks toward the uncertain future that awaits. If properly understood and managed, psychodramatic closure conveys the truism that even as something ends, it begins again and again and again. That's about the only thing we can be sure of.

This is as true of the closure at the end of a session or the life of a group as it is of the closure at the end of an individual psychodrama.

8

SHARING: PSYCHODRAMA IN CONTEXT

The Supporting Infrastructure of Psychodrama

I n the context of psychotherapeutic practice, psychodramatists of repute are likely to be members of professional organizations which govern the discipline and offer definitions of safe, ethical practice. For the most part, these organizations are national bodies that in some way recognize psychodrama practitioners and psychodramatists in training and publish codes of ethics and practice to which practising members must adhere. These codes establish guidelines for practitioners, trainers and supervisors of psychodrama and, perhaps more importantly, set standards by which consumers of their services can determine whether they have been treated properly. No codes of ethics and practice can offer guarantees but they can and do offer a means of redress in the event of bad practice. Any potential psychodrama client or psychodrama trainee would be well advised to check that the practice of the practitioner or trainer with whom they wish to work is governed by a published code and that it is freely available. Some organizations (for example the British Psychodrama Association) register trainees, practitioners and trainers. Inclusion on these registers indicates that the member reaches specified standards, subscribes to the organization's relevant codes and is of good standing. In the event of any allegation of malpractice, there is recourse to the investigatory and disciplinary procedures of the registering organization. In the United

Kingdom, there is a further guarantee because the British Psychodrama Association (BPA) is a constituent member of the United Kingdom Council for Psychotherapy (UKCP), belonging to its Humanistic and Integrative Psychotherapies Section (HIPS). Psychodramatists on the practitioner and trainer registers of the BPA may therefore also choose to register as psychodrama psychotherapists with the UKCP and are then additionally governed by its codes and procedures. The UKCP publishes annually a list of all its registered members. This register contains entries by region and by section, it may be purchased and it is available in (for example) larger public libraries. The UKCP register may be a starting place for anyone in the UK seeking to contact a reputable psychodramatist.

To be recognized and perhaps registered as a psychodrama practitioner, members must be able to demonstrate that they have met the training requirements of the organization and that they continue to meet any other criteria set for safe practice. These criteria vary but they are likely to include a commitment to ongoing training and some reference to the need for pyschodramatists to regularly review their practice with a supervisor or consultant. There may also be a requirement that the psychodramatist practises for at least a minimum number of hours per year.

Besides registering psychodrama practitioners, constituting codes for safe, ethical practice and administering complaints and disciplinary procedures, professional organizations have other purposes. Their major function is to promote psychodrama and the interests of psychodramatists and their clients. For example, the American Society for Group Psychotherapy and Psychodrama publishes its mission statement on the World Wide Web (**http://www.artswire.org/asgpp/**). This is:

1 To foster the national and international cooperation among all who are concerned with the theory and practice of psychodrama, sociometry and group psychotherapy.
2 To encourage and promote professional training in psychodrama, sociometry and group psychotherapy.
3 To promote the spread and fruitful application of theories and methods of psychodrama, sociometry and group psychotherapy in professional disciplines concerned with the well-being of individuals, groups, families and organizations.

4 To disseminate information about psychodrama, sociometry and group psychotherapy and their applications to the general public, other professionals and public policy-makers.
5 To promote and publish research in psychodrama, sociometry and group psychotherapy, and related fields.
6 To maintain a code of professional standards relevant to the purposes of the Society.

The aims of other organizations are similar and they seek to achieve them in many ways. They may publish academic journals, for example, the BPA is responsible for the *British Journal of Psychodrama and Sociodrama*, the American Society for Group Psychotherapy and Psychodrama publishes the *International Journal of Action Methods* (formerly the *Journal of Group Psychotherapy, Psychodrama and Sociometry*). There is also the *Australia and New Zealand Psychodrama Association Journal* and journals in many languages other than English.

Some psychodrama associations are themselves training organizations, others are umbrella organizations to which training organizations may belong. Whichever is the case, the psychodrama organizations usually have a part to play in establishing and maintaining criteria for training and monitoring the progress of students. For example, the BPA, through its accreditation committee, agrees and disseminates standards for training and assessment and monitors the content and delivery of the programmes of its constituent training organizations to ensure that these standards are met. The American Society for Group Psychotherapy and Psychodrama (ASGPP) serves a similar function in the USA and (at **http://www.artswire.org/asgpp/cert6.html**) sets out its requirements for practitioner certification. These are essentially similar to the standards of, for example, the BPA. At the same web site, the ASGPP also sets forth its requirements for certification as a trainer, educator, practitioner (TEP), which is a qualification recognizing the senior status of its holders.

Many psychodrama associations organize regular conferences, usually annually. These may have a 'business' component, perhaps in the form of the association's annual general meeting, but they normally also comprise a series of presented papers and experiential workshops addressing psychodrama and its allied disciplines. The intention of such conferences is to offer psychodramatists and trainees an opportunity for on-going training and professional updating, but they are often open to non-members and can form a valuable introduction to the discipline. Occasionally, there are international psychodrama conferences but, as yet, there is no organization with the responsibility to organize them and it is usually national organizations or groups of individuals who take on this task. The International Association of Group Psychotherapy (IAGP) has a special interest group for psychodrama, the International Psychodrama Section (IPS). Psychodrama is also represented at the International Congress of Group Psychotherapy and at the World Conference for Psychotherapy.

Psychodrama organizations may also coordinate and/or collate information about the activities of their members. For example, *BPA News* (the house journal of the BPA) regularly publishes details of training opportunities and where and when psychodrama psychotherapy may be offered, although these lists are not exhaustive. However, anyone intending to train as a psychodramatist or who wishes to experience psychodrama for themselves may find the information they need through the professional organization covering the country or area in which they live.

Psychodrama Training

Blatner (1997: 203–214) publishes an 'International Directory of Psychodrama Training Institutes' in which there are over 150 entries (with addresses); this does not include opportunities in the USA where, Blatner states, there are over 100 trainers who are listed in the directory of the American Board of Examiners in Psychodrama, Sociometry and Group Psychotherapy, which is published annually. There are psychodrama training organizations or individual psychodrama trainers in at least thirty countries, including: Argentina, Australia, Austria, Belgium, Brazil, Bulgaria, Canada, Eire, Finland, France, Germany, Greece, Hungary, Israel, Japan, Italy, Korea, Netherlands, New Zealand, Norway, Portugal, Romania, Russia, Spain, Sweden, Switzerland, Taiwan, Turkey, the United Kingdom and the United States of America.

Psychodrama training is at a postgraduate level. This does not always mean that trainee psychodramatists must hold a first degree but, if they do not, then a professional qualification of some kind (for example, in social work, nursing or some other approach to counselling or psychotherapy) is normally expected. For example, the Psychodrama Training Institute of South Australia (which adheres to the standards set by the Australia and New Zealand Psychodrama Association) publishes its criteria for eligibility to train on the World Wide Web. These can be found at **http://www.holistic.com.au/ptisa/index.html**:

> Courses are suitable for practitioners established in their work and who have a relevant tertiary qualification or equivalent. The training is 'postgraduate'.
>
> Such practitioners may apply psychodrama in many different areas in which people are learning, changing and relating to others, in management, public relations, training, education, healing, spiritual life, business, performing arts and in organizations.
>
> All those who value a thoughtful and purposive approach to quality interactions with people are likely to benefit from some involvement in this training.

Clearly, the training offered here is much broader than psychodrama as psychotherapy alone. Some training organizations may restrict their endeavours to psychodrama psychotherapy and prospective students must ensure that the institutions they approach offer training that will meet their needs.

In most cases, applicants for psychodrama psychotherapy training are expected to have some experience of mental health work, and in some countries membership of the professional psychodrama organizations (for example the Sociedade Portuguesa de Psicodrama), is restricted to people who are also psychiatrists or clinical psychologists – this implies a similar restriction on training in psychodrama psychotherapy. There is also often a requirement that prospective students have some experience of psychodrama psychotherapy in the client role.

The exact nature of psychodrama training varies but it usually comprises a large experiential element. As well as theoretical studies of psychodrama, sociometry, group psychotherapy and related disciplines, psychodrama students participate in actual psychodramas from an early stage. In psychodrama training groups, procedures are essentially the same as in groups for clients; trainees are expected to offer themselves as protagonists (presenting personal material) and auxiliaries and to participate in sharing. Senior students will also be expected to direct enactments under the supervision of the trainers. The major difference between training groups and therapy or growth groups is that, in the former, sharing is followed by a fourth element known as *processing*.

The purpose of processing is to analyse and evaluate the performance of the director so that all may learn. Kellerman (1992: 161) sees that 'the main purpose of processing is to improve the professional skills of students in training'. Some trainers encourage the processing of sessions which they have directed themselves (so that students may get a better understanding of the actions of the trainer and the reasons for those actions), but what makes psychodrama processing particularly valuable is that it offers the student director feedback on work which has actually been witnessed by trainers and peers (including the protagonist and the auxiliaries). Wheresoever practicably possible, processing is separated from sharing by at least a short interval. Many trainers prefer to leave the processing of a session until later in the day or even until the next day. This is because, whereas sharing is a continuation of the therapeutic endeavour, processing is, by definition, likely to contain a critical element which sits ill with the accepting climate needed for good therapy. Group members (and especially the protagonist) benefit from time in which to detach themselves emotionally from the session and to consolidate its effects. Kellerman (1992: 161–167) gives a good account of psychodrama processing.

Training in psychodrama also requires senior students to complete a period of supervised clinical practice. This requirement is usually that, in the course of a given period, the trainee directs between 60 and 90 sessions (as pre-determined by the accrediting organization). These sessions must be discussed and processed with a clinical supervisor. This clinical practice follows on from a specified minimum period of training and can commence only with the trainer's approval. The assessment of psychodrama training normally comprises an appraisal of both theoretical knowledge and practical skill. The way in which this is done varies: for example, in the UK and Australia/New Zealand, theoretical knowledge is largely continually assessed (students submit essays at least the last of which should be 'of a publishable standard'), whereas in the USA there is a formal written examination. The ability of candidates to conduct a full psychodrama session is normally assessed by on-site examination by an approved examiner. National organizations may be able to supply exact details of the nature of psychodrama training locally and the addresses of trainers and training organizations.

In Britain, accredited psychodrama training is available from:

Institution	Contact address
Hoewell International Centre for Psychodrama	North Walk, Lynton, North Devon, EX35 6HL
London Centre of Psychodrama & Group Psychotherapy	15 Audley Road, Richmond, TW10 6EY
The Northern School of Psychodrama	The Registrar, Northern School of Psychodrama, Glebe Cottage, Church Road, Mellor, Stockport, SK6 5LX
Oxford Psychodrama Group	8 Rahere Road, Cowley, Oxford, OX4 3QG
South Devon College of Arts and Technology	Dorothy Langley, Dept of Music and Theatre Arts, Newton Road, Torquay, TQ2 5BY

Working as a Psychodramatist

Where and how trained psychodramatists deploy and employ their skills differs greatly. In the UK, there are very few people employed as psychodramatists although there are many others who use their psychodrama skills in the course of their employment as, for example, psychiatric nurses, psychologists or educators. The web site of the Psychodrama Institute of South Australia suggests that psychodrama training is appropriate for 'leaders, managers, therapists, group workers, nurses, doctors, educators, teachers, counsellors, pastors, psychologists and administrators', which implies that each of these will find psychodrama useful in their existing roles. Most psychodramatists who operate as psychotherapists do so either in health care institutions (where they are likely to use their psychodrama skills as an adjunct to other skills) or in private practice. In many countries, only qualified psychiatrists and psychologists may practise as psychotherapists and this applies to psychodrama psychotherapists as much as any others. In (for example) the UK, there is no such restriction on psychodrama as therapy and the non-clinical use of psychodrama (in, for example, teaching or management) is generally unrestricted.

Joining a Psychodrama Group

Perhaps the first question for which any prospective psychodrama client needs an answer is, 'Is psychodrama right for me at this time?' In the final analysis, only the client can provide the answer and it would be impossible to describe a 'typical' psychodrama client. Psychodrama is an approach to growth and psychotherapy which is used with all sorts of people in all sorts of settings. Kellerman (1992: 23) states:

> From one point of view, all people can benefit from psychodrama at various times in their life cycles, particularly when in emotional distress. From another point of view, there is a category of people for whom psychodrama is the treatment of choice – and yet there is no way to identify these people.

Kellerman indicates that while people with a large range of mental health problems may benefit from psychodrama, not everybody does. This is less to do with the nature of the 'problem' and more to do with the person in relation to psychodrama or the setting in which it is conducted. In my experience, a properly informed prospective client will almost always know if psychodrama is the right approach for them. Once again, trusting the client seems the obvious strategy.

Although psychodrama is 'an action method', members of a psychodrama group are not required to have acting skills. What is important is that they are willing to encounter the other members of the group and to work with them and the group leader for the benefit of all. This does not require a spirit of self-sacrifice; each group member has their own aims and can legitimately expect to address them except where to do so would be to the detriment of another. Kellerman (1992: 23) states some necessary qualities for psychodrama clients:

> Naturally, psychodrama can be helpful only to those individuals who are able and motivated to participate in the rather complex psychic rituals which characterise this approach. The ability, for example, to participate in the imaginary process of role playing without losing touch with outer reality seems to be a minimal requirement for participation. Furthermore, participants must be able to experience surges of feelings without loss of impulse control, have at least some capacity to establish interpersonal relations, have a minimal tolerance for anxiety and frustration (ego strength), some psychological mindedness, and a capacity for adaptive regression in the service of the ego.

Anyone considering experiencing psychodrama for themselves should consult the section 'Finding a Psychodrama Psychotherapist and the Shape of Psychodrama' in Chapter 2.

Finding Out More about Psychodrama

In line with the psychodrama director's request of the protagonist 'Don't tell us, show us', the best way of finding out more about psychodrama is actually to experience it as a group member. Whether this is in a regular group, on a weekend intensive or at a training conference is a matter of personal choice and availability. That said, there are now many psychodrama publications to which the interested reader can refer. These include Moreno's own works, books and papers about him, academic journals in most European and some Asian languages and books by practitioners of many stripes. A guide to further reading may be found in Appendix 2. Increasingly, the Internet is also a source of information about psychodrama.

Psychodrama and the Internet

When asked to find 'psychodrama', the major search engines turn up more than six hundred entries on the Internet. Even allowing for the fact that this includes some rather strange pages where psychodrama is understood in some colloquial sense which has little direct connection with the ideas and practices of Moreno, this is an impressive (and growing) number. These entries include those for individual practitioners, trainers, training institutions, national and international organizations and journals. There are also pages that introduce psychodrama theory, those that give details of forthcoming conferences and those that provide connections to related disciplines and interests. There are pages in many languages, including Finnish, French, Italian and Portuguese, although it appears that (after English) German is the most common. Finding a way through this labyrinth can be difficult and reference to one of the 'psychodrama link' pages may save time and energy. On the other hand, surfing from one connection to another allows for serendipitous discovery. Some potentially useful web addresses are given below.

At **http://merlin.net.au/~iam/pdlinks.html** there is Robert Brodie's 'Psychodrama Links' page, which is frequently updated and which leads to all manner of interesting and useful psychodrama pages.

The Western Institute for Focused Action Therapy, of Phoenix, Arizona, also provides a 'Psychodrama Links' page at **http://www.syspac.com/~casa/pdlinks.html**
National and international organizations with web pages include:

The American Society of Group Psychotherapy and Psychodrama at:
http://www.artswire.org/asgpp/cert6.html

The British Psychodrama Association at:
**http://www.zambula.demon.co.uk/
application%20info.html**
(This page also leads to information about Hoewell-by-the-Sea International Centre for Psychodrama which is run by Marcia Karp and Ken Sprague.)

The Finnish Psychodrama Association (in Finnish) at:
http://www.sci.fi/~suomenpd/pdrykoti.html

The International Psychodrama Section of the International Association for Group Psychotherapy at:
http://www.psych.mcgill.ca/labs/iagp/Kipper.html

The Portuguese Psychodrama Association (Sociedade Portuguesa de Psicodrama) at:
http://members.tripod.com/~cristinv/spp.html

At **http://www.mhsource.com/edu/psytimes/p950520.html**
Adam Blatner provides a short introduction to 'Psychodramatic Methods in Psychotherapy'.

Anne Schutzenberger's Home Page (in French) provides (amongst other things) details of forthcoming psychodrama events throughout the world at **http://perso.wanadoo.fr/a.ancelin.
schutzenberger/html**

9

PROCESSING: A CRITICAL LOOK AT PSYCHODRAMA

'Effectiveness' and Evaluation: Psychodrama and Research

Any potential psychodrama client or psychodrama student can quite legitimately ask 'Does psychodrama work?' As a psychodramatist, I have the evidence of my own eyes and my own experience as a member of psychodrama groups, the experiences of my colleagues and the stories of psychodrama clients, all of which convince me that it does. This anecdotal evidence is powerful but it falls a long way short of the 'proof' which might be expected of scientific studies nor is it as convincing as the 'intensive, authentic descriptive accounts of experience and action' (McLeod, 1994: 32) which are the goal of qualitative research. Nor do anecdotes do any more than imply for whom, when and where psychodrama is effective or valued or what is helpful about it. Where is the research evidence for the effectiveness of psychodrama?

As Karp (1995: 297) indicates, the findings of research into group psychotherapy *per se* may be applicable to psychodrama but, although such studies may be helpful to an understanding of (for example) group process, with respect to effectiveness there is a great deal of ambiguity. Bloch (1988: 299–308) doubts that the question 'Is group therapy effective?' is worth asking because 'group therapy' is a term embracing all sorts of approaches and because it does not take account of the idea of for whom group therapy might be effective. In a comparison with individual therapy, Orlinsky and Howard (1978: 310–311) report that the great majority of outcome studies addressing the relative efficacy of group therapy show no significant differences between the two. However, they also state that some studies have found that group psychotherapy is significantly better than individual therapy and that two studies indicate that a combination is favoured. As far as I can determine, none of the studies to which these authors refer was on psychodrama and, while it is *likely* that findings can be generalized, their relevance is open to question and any connection unproven. Studies of group therapy *per se* can only take us so far in an understanding of how psychodrama 'works'. Also, psychodramatists argue that their approach is unique – it offers something other approaches do not. This claim too is worthy of investigation and substantiation can only come from research into the theory and practice of psychodrama itself.

In their bibliography of psychodrama, Sacks et al. (1995) list only thirty works under 'research', and I (Wilkins, 1997a: 44) noted 'there are few studies of psychodrama which demonstrate its usefulness or value, examine the client experience or address advances in theory or practice.' Torres (1998: 2) also comments on 'the lack of visibility' of psychodrama with respect to other approaches to psychotherapy. He writes:

> This lack of visibility results from a small interest of psychodramatists in general in research and/or in publishing their results in generalist psychological or medical journals. But it is also true that we [psychodramatists] make little effort to answer questions like the efficacy of psychodramatic treatments, the indications and contra-indications, the failures, the alternative handling for specific psychopathological conditions, etc., or to add some kind of scientific evidence to our answers.

McLeod (1994: 183) suggests that psychotherapy practitioners in general are critical of therapy research. Psychodramatists are no exception to this, especially when research is equated with positivistic investigations:

> It is as if psychodramatists do not see themselves as having the skills necessary for research. . . . We see our expertise in creative, intuitive and imaginative processes and our interest in human experience as antipathetic to research. (Wilkins, 1997a: 44)

Although papers presenting the results of systematic quantitative or qualitative investigations of psychodrama are rare, there are, however, many which present the subjective accounts of practitioners working with many different client groups and in many settings. In these papers, psychodramatists are writing of their thoughts as 'reflective practitioners' which can be viewed as a 'first step' on the ladder of research (see Wilkins, 1997b: 8–9) but lacking the rigour and the reliability of quantitative research or the authenticity of qualitative approaches. They are, however, of great value to anyone wishing to know more about psychodrama and the ways in which it is practised. The importance of the practitioner in the development of psychodrama cannot be over-rated. As McLeod (1994: 184) points out:

> All the key figures in the development of psychotherapy (Freud, Jung, Rogers, Perls, Moreno, Wolpe, Ellis, Beck) made their important discoveries in the clinic, even if some of them then went on to test the validity of these discoveries through systematic research.

For the most part, those systematic studies of psychodrama which have been published are by practitioners. For example, Kellerman (1985, 1987b) has used questionnaires to investigate the perception clients have of the 'therapeutic factors in psychodrama' and Bradbury (1995b) used a quantitative approach to measure change as the result of psychodrama psychotherapy. Other recent quantitative studies include an investigation of the effects of psychodrama on prison inmates (Stallone, 1993) in which (using the number of 'institutional disciplinary reports' as a measure of change) the author reports (p. 29):

> The results of this study suggest that psychodrama may have played a significant role in reducing the unacceptable behaviours of the inmates who participated in the psychodrama group and in promoting their positive adjustment to life in prison.

There are also some papers in which the research methodology is 'psychodramatic' in the broad sense. For example, Ben-David (1992) used sociometry in a study of leadership in psychotherapeutic groups, Drew (1993) describes 're-enactment interviewing', which she says borrows from the psychodramatic method and Hawkins (1988: 60–78) has written about a particular use of psychodrama as research. What is largely missing from the psychodrama literature is reports of good qualitative research, especially research from a humanistic or 'new paradigm' perspective (see Reason and Rowan, 1981). This is in the process of change. For example, there are on-going studies of the client experience of person-centred psychodrama (Wilkins, in press) and what it is about psychodrama that people who hear voices find helpful (Casson, personal communication, 1996).

With respect to an understanding of psychodrama, neither quantitative, positivistic methods nor humanistic, phenomenological methods are to be preferred. Both approaches (and others) have something to contribute and it may be that they are best used in combination – certainly they can complement one another. Moreno (1968: 3) wrote:

> The question as to the validity of psychodrama has aroused consider-able controversy in the course of the years. There have been two opinions. One emphasizes that the usual measures of reliability and validity do not seem to be particularly appropriate for psychodrama. If each person acts out his life honestly, the data are perfectly reliable and valid. The second opinion is that the current methods for measuring validity can be applied. The two opinions do not exclude one another. The two methods of validation ('existential' and 'scientific') can be combined.

The task of combining these two approaches to research (or at least collating their respective findings) remains. In this psycho-drama is not unique among psychotherapies, but the absence of a well-grounded research tradition does psychodrama no favours and exposes it to criticism which might otherwise be more easily rebutted.

Resistances to Psychodrama

Moreno is a significant figure in the development of psychotherapy. He developed techniques and practices which are widely used in other approaches to psychotherapy and psychodrama can be viewed as the forerunner of group psychotherapy. Corey (1994: 229) acknowledges this:

> In many ways psychodrama was the precursor of many other group approaches, including Gestalt therapy, family therapy, encounter, and some applications of behavior-therapy groups. These orientations often use techniques that were originally developed by J.L. Moreno or adap-tations.

and goes on to state (p. 232):

> The more I learn about the techniques that Moreno pioneered, the more aware I become of his genius as a practitioner. It is an understatement to say that he was ahead of his time. With his visionary perspective he created methods for integrating feelings, fantasies, and actions.

I and many others share Corey's experience and his view. Given this extraordinary range of influence, Moreno's own contributions to psychotherapy should occupy a prominent place and yet psy-chodrama and its related disciplines are far less widely practised and less understood than his status as an innovator, thinker and creator suggests. Blatner with Blatner (1988: 32) write, 'the work of J.L. Moreno has great potential but has not been widely accepted in the United States'. Although there may have been a partial shift, ten years later this remains true, and it is equally true of (for example) the United Kingdom, where, many years after its foundation, a chapter on psychodrama appeared in a book on 'innovative therapies' (see Badaines, 1988). This suggests that psychodrama is in some sense outside of the mainstream.

Blatner with Blatner (1988: 32–42) write of 'resistances to psychodrama' and attribute this neglect of Moreno's ideas to the fact that his concepts were ahead of his time and that he 'behaved in ways that alienated a large number of his fellow professionals'. They also list the historical factors on which the resistance to psychodrama is based. These include:

1   That it departed radically from the accepted modes of psychotherapeutic practice.
2   That, as the practice of psychotherapy expanded into innovative areas, the connections with psychodrama were largely ignored.
3   Moreno's practice of contrasting himself with the dominant ideology of psychoanalysis won him few friends.
4   The time necessary for a psychodrama session made it less suitable for clinical practice, where the '50-minute hour' had become the norm and, additionally, that psychodrama is emotionally stirring means that more aftercare and support may be needed for psychodrama clients than for (for example) clients in analysis.
5   Assumptions were made that psychodrama was directive and authoritarian in its approach to clients. By the mid-1930s this had become unfashionable.
6   There is a prejudice against being active in therapy.
7   The theatrical form (from which Moreno borrowed language and ideas) is seen by some as inherently inauthentic. This association leads to a distrust of psychodrama.
8   Over the years, psychodrama has been practised by people without proper training – this has reflected on the method rather than the untrained directors.
9   Group approaches have been unfashionable and, although this is changing, 'even today, people are instinctively wary of

action methods because the conventional defence systems of verbal interchange are superseded'.

10 Therapists have been inadequately prepared (socially or professionally) to cope with groups.

11 In its traditional form, psychodrama was originally difficult to learn and to apply. Only Moreno offered training in psychodrama. This limited the number of practitioners and therefore the impact of psychodrama.

Blatner with Blatner (1988: 37–41) discuss the personal attributes and behaviours of Moreno which contributed to resistance to his philosophy and therefore the practice of psychodrama. Briefly, these include:

1 That, in a number of ways, his inclusiveness was seen as 'unprofessional' by other psychotherapists.

2 That the written material addressing psychodrama was limited and (until the mid-1960s) almost solely produced by Moreno. Although when it is studied carefully this work is internally consistent, it is difficult to understand, and 'his querulous tone discouraged the development of a serious professional audience'. Moreno also missed the opportunity to compare his ideas with other approaches, which may have made them more accessible.

3 Moreno concentrated the publishing of psychodrama in his own hands, largely ignoring the professional journals. This limited readership and, because articles sometimes lacked rigour, 'diminished the general credibility of the journals themselves'.

4 Moreno's way of presenting himself sometimes offended. He was charismatic but could also be experienced as grandiose or even megalomaniac. When he spoke, he was often inspiring to many but others found him unprofessional, 'simply boring, irrelevant, or "off-the-wall" '.

5 Although he had the characteristics of a 'true healer', Moreno could also be 'petty, insensitive, arrogant, capricious, overly controlling, and fairly narcissistic.' Collaborating with Moreno was not easy and rarely repeated. It seems that although he influenced many people and was respected and held in affection by his students, Moreno made few close friends and 'with experience one learned to stay somewhat wary'.

6 Moreno's determination to control the dissemination of his ideas was counter-productive and contributed to the lack of understanding and isolation of traditional psychodrama.

Although many of these obstacles have been at least partly overcome, the residual effects still influence the practice of psychodrama which is increasingly finding its proper place in the world. Zerka Moreno is optimistic that Moreno's time will come again. In Hare and Hare (1996: vii) she writes: 'For a while, social scientists listened to [Moreno's] voice, then he was absorbed and submerged by the culture. I believe he will be rediscovered.'

Blatner with Blatner (1988: 41–42) pay tribute to Moreno and Zerka Moreno thus:

> After considering the many difficulties involved, it is a tribute to Moreno's strengths of courage, persistence, and vision that his approach has survived as well as it has. A great deal of credit must go to his wife, Zerka, who moderated many of his faults and championed his work, both before and after his death. . . .
>
> The major reason Moreno's ideas continue to stimulate professionals in a number of fields is that they are basically valid, powerful, and relevant, now more than ever.

This is undoubtedly true, but powerful ideas are not sufficient of themselves and psychodrama needs to be effectively presented and authenticated for it to overcome the remnants of prejudice arising from the resistances described by Blatner with Blatner. As they write (1988: 42):

> For a system to be accepted . . . it is not enough for it to contain excellent ideas and powerful techniques. It must also be established as theoretically clear and coherent, professionally reputable, and scientifically effective. Otherwise, it will seem to be just a 'gimmick'.

Criticisms of Psychodrama

Psychodrama is susceptible to criticisms of psychotherapy *per se* but also attracts its own peculiar criticisms, some of which arise out of the resistances listed above. Many others centre around the use of action rather than words and especially the fear that encouraging people to engage with their emotional history as if it were in the present is disruptive and disturbing. Hare and Hare (1996: 89–91) adapt some of the commonly held reservations about psychodrama listed by Blatner in 1968 and give rebuttals:

1   A fear of *acting out* associated with the meaning of action in psychodrama.
    Rebuttal: 'Acting out' is generally conceptualised as an antitherapeutic discharge of neurotic tensions through behaviour which repeats an unconscious situation instead of remembering fully with

the appropriate attending emotions. In psychodrama, the remembering is enacted rather than only verbalised, as in free association. Further, the enactment takes place in the context of group therapy, where the enactment is subject to the observing and analysing functions of the ego of the protagonist.

2   A fear that enactment may produce overwhelming *anxiety* and *precipitate psychosis* or violent behaviour.
    Rebuttal: As in verbal therapies, the problem is not whether to generate anxiety, but rather how to structure this essential process in therapy. The channelling of anxiety is done through the use of proper timing and maintaining coping strategies. Further, a cohesive and confident group can be reassuring to a protagonist who fears loss of control.

3   A criticism that psychodrama seems *unnatural*.
    Rebuttal: All therapies are different from the everyday experience of the patient. Psychotherapy helps a patient re-experience life and interaction in a new light. Although a patient may be more familiar with verbal methods, since this is the norm for the psychoanalytic tradition, once experienced, the richness of the world of action, emotion, and imagination becomes apparent.

4   A concern that psychodrama is *directive*.
    Rebuttal: To be directive by asking the protagonist to try out some activity is not the same as imposing a focus of investigation or some interpretation upon the patient. The psychodrama director can fully respect the protagonist's choice of a situation to explore even in the most structured of psychodramas.

5   A reservation about the usefulness of *action rather than verbal methods* to clarify group views.
    Rebuttal: A group with communication difficulties may not be able to deal with intragroup conflicts by verbal discussion. Often only a shared experience, through the use of action methods, can provide a focus to which all can relate so that different expectations and attitudes can be clarified.

6   A perception of action techniques as *gimmicky*, that the use of 'techniques' is incompatible with developing an 'honest and genuine relationship' with the patient.
    Rebuttal: If the technique is used in an open manner, is explicit, is time-limited, and is related to the enactment and not the therapeutic relationship, then the therapist is being neither insincere nor ambiguous.

7   Reservations from persons who have only seen psychodrama being directed by *insufficiently trained* directors when psychodrama seems boring to the audience or awkward or destructive for the protagonist.
    Rebuttal: The problem is not with psychodrama but with the director. A director should use a proper warm-up, often involving a great deal of movement. A director should not assign roles to the protagonist which are unfamiliar or too emotionally loaded. A

director should ensure a supportive atmosphere in the group, through 'sharing' and other methods, otherwise a poorly timed interpretation can lead to a distressing loss of self-esteem for the protagonist.

8 A criticism that regards the involvement of the *use of role as artificial* and that taking a role leads to phoney or game-like behaviour.

Rebuttal: The concept of role is compatible with a model of humans as involved, spontaneous, and fully self-actualising beings.

9 A suspicion that *enactment creates distortion* of the protagonist's conflict, thus rendering the method invalid.

Rebuttal: The same criticism can apply to a verbal therapist since the reconstruction of past events is subject to the censorship of the patient. However, action involves more of the senses in remembering and a greater involvement, which reduces defensive manoeuvres that distort the revelation of a historical event.

10 A criticism of the *lack of controlled experimental studies* in the field.

Rebuttal: Blatner does not offer a rebuttal; writing in 1968, he agrees that the psychodrama method awaits the validation of properly controlled outcome studies.

Thirty years after Blatner first made this list, it still has validity and relevance. The fear that psychodrama will provoke emotional distress, perhaps even to a dangerous degree, is particularly widespread. This is perhaps an instinctive acknowledgement of the potency of enactment as a vehicle for change and may reflect cultural taboos about the public display of emotion. In my experience, people who actually witness psychodrama, even if sceptical at the outset, usual come round to the idea that, in the hands of a trained and proficient psychodramatist, it is safe. Hare and Hare (1996: 91–93) review some of the evidence supporting the safety of psychodrama. This evidence indicates that psychodrama does not induce psychotic behaviour and that 'fragile' clients are relatively safe in the hands of a competent practitioner. Where loss of control does occur, this can be contained without harmful effects and it may provide the opportunity for therapeutic intervention. Other evidence they cite suggests that proper training is essential for the safe practice of psychodrama.

Psychodrama is not a panacea for all human ills. From anecdotal evidence, we know that many people, of many kinds, in many settings *can* benefit from psychodrama when the practitioner is well-trained and professionally competent. We know too that its techniques can be powerful and they are not suitable for everybody

– their use requires sound clinical judgement and a deep sensitivity to the protagonist on the part of the director. Given these conditions, there are answers to many of the criticisms of psychodrama but some remain unanswered.

Like many approaches to psychotherapy, psychodrama can be criticized because the research evidence for its effectiveness is limited. In terms of research findings, little is known of how the techniques of psychodrama 'work', what therapist characteristics are required of a successful psychodramatist, how psychodrama can best be delivered, for whom it is an unsuitable modality and just what its consumers value. All this has direct bearing upon the status of psychodrama in professional and public sectors. It is only as psychodramatists publish more of the results of their work in mainstream professional journals that they will gain professional credibility. Only when psychodrama is seen as contributing significantly to the practice of psychotherapy and as having something unique to offer that is effective and valued by clients will other professionals consider referring people for psychodrama psychotherapy. The resulting higher profile of psychodrama would attract more clients and more students to psychodrama training.

Appendix 1

GLOSSARY OF PSYCHODRAMA TERMS

Act hunger: The conscious or unconscious need to give expression to emotional tension through enaction.

Audience: All those members of a psychodrama group who are not directly involved in an enactment as protagonist, auxiliaries or director.

Auxiliary or **Auxiliary ego:** A group member who is (usually) chosen by the protagonist to take a role in a psychodrama enactment.

Creativity: One of the cornerstones of psychodrama theory (the other is spontaneity). To be creative is to respond constructively to new situations. Creativity is an innate human characteristic which can become blocked. Psychodrama is a way of freeing these blocks.

Co-therapy/co-therapist: When two therapists work together leading a group as equals, they are co-therapists. Sometimes 'co-therapist' refers to a junior member of such a team, the other being called 'therapist', but this usage is increasingly unusual.

Director: The person who works with the protagonist to guide the course of a psychodrama. Loosely, the leader of a psychodrama group.

Doubling/double: When another group member joins the protagonist, taking on their posture and, when it is helpful, speaking for the protagonist, they are said to be a double. Doubles are of two kinds. Permanent doubles serve a supportive function and may be at the protagonist's side throughout an enactment, spontaneous doubles are members of the audience who, with the consent of the protagonist and the director, temporarily enter a scene and, speaking as if with the protagonist's voice, offer their sense of something which the protagonist is unable to express.

Enaction: The phase of a psychodrama, normally comprising several scenes real or imagined, past, present or future, in which protagonists spontaneously act out some aspect of their life story.

Encounter: The true meeting of individuals; the process of seeing another as they see themselves; authentic social relations. In psychodrama, encounter is greatly aided by role reversal.

Mirroring: A process in which the protagonist's part in the drama is taken by another who then does and says what the protagonist did previously while the latter watches. This 'instant replay' allows the protagonist a more objective view of the scene.

Processing: The critical evaluation of directors and their actions by other members of the group in psychodrama training groups. This follows after sharing, from which it is clearly separated, usually by the elapse of time.

Protagonist: The person who is the focus of a particular psychodrama chosen in some way from the group to enact some aspect of their story.

Role reversal: When protagonists take on the role of 'the other' in their dramas and the auxiliary plays the protagonist, roles are said to be reversed.

Scene-setting: Where the protagonist and director work together using objects (and sometimes people) in the room to establish the physical environment of the forthcoming enaction on the psychodrama stage.

Sharing: The last phase in psychodrama psychotherapy, following directly after the enactment. In sharing, each member of the group has the opportunity to tell the protagonist what experiences and feelings they share with them.

Social atom: An individual's immediate social network. Originally the social network into which a person is born and which continues to affect them throughout life, but also used to mean those 'significant others' surrounding an individual in the present.

Sociatry: A therapy for social ills, that is, the use of psychodramatic and group therapeutic techniques to heal social structures.

Sociodrama: The exploration of social issues through the use of psychodramatic techniques. As psychodrama is to individuals, so sociodrama is to social groups.

Sociometry: An approach to the measurement of interpersonal relationships.

Spontaneity: With creativity from which it springs, one of the linchpins of psychodrama and essential to healthy living; defined by Moreno as a new response to an old situation or an adequate (that is appropriate) response to a new one.

Stage: The physical setting of a psychodrama enactment. This may be a specifically allocated or designed area or selected in some way by the protagonist.

Surplus reality: A psychodramatic space in which scenes that, as Zerka Moreno is credited with saying, 'have never happened, will never happen, or can never happen' are enacted and for which there is a psychological or emotional need.

Tele: In simple terms, a form of mutual empathy. A quality of interpersonal preference in which there is reprocity and a sense of connectedness.

Vignette: A short, focused piece of psychodramatic work usually comprising only one unelaborated scene.

Warm-up: The first phase of psychodrama in which the group and the therapist work together to develop group cohesion and to prepare to enter a psychological/emotional exploration.

Appendix 2

A GUIDE TO FURTHER READING

A Selection of Works by J.L. Moreno (and his collaborators):

Psychodrama, Volume I (4th edn), Amber, PA: Beacon House, 1985.

Psychodrama, Volume II: *Foundations of Psychotherapy* (with Z.T. Moreno), Beacon, NY: Beacon House, 1975.

Psychodrama, Volume III: *Action Therapy and Principles of Practice* (with Z.T. Moreno), Beacon, NY: Beacon House, 1975.

Who Shall Survive? Foundations of Sociometry, Group Psychotherapy and Sociodrama, Beacon, NY: Beacon House, 1953.

Moreno wrote more than fifty major books and articles, either as sole author or in collaboration with others. The above four books can be considered as the classic works of psychodrama. They are not always easy reading but they do contain Moreno's major contributions in his own words.

Books About J.L. Moreno

J.L. Moreno (A.P. and J.R. Hare), London: Sage, 1996 (in the series *Key Figures in Counselling and Psychotherapy*).

Jacob Levy Moreno 1889–1974: Father of Psychodrama, Sociometry, and Group Psychotherapy (R.F. Marineau), London: Routledge, 1989.

A Selection of English Language Books on Psychodrama

Acting-In: Practical Applications of Psychodramatic Methods, 3rd edn (A. Blatner), New York: Springer, 1996.

A practical guide to psychodrama techniques aimed at students updated to take account of recent developments.

Focus on Psychodrama: The Therapeutic Aspects of Psychodrama (P.F. Kellerman), London: Jessica Kingsley, 1992.

A book in which psychodrama practice is strongly related to theory.

Forbidden Agendas: Strategic Action in Groups (A. Williams), London: Routledge, 1991.

A practical text which 'recommends a new approach to groupwork, based on systems theory and dramatic action'.

Foundations of Psychodrama: History, Theory and Practice (A. Blatner, with A. Blatner), New York: Springer, 1988.

A companion to *Acting-In*, which addresses the historical, philosophical, psychological, social and practical foundations of psychodrama.

The Inner World Outside: Object Relations Theory and Psychodrama (P. Holmes), London: Routledge, 1992.

The author introduces object relations theory and relates it to psychodrama through the use of examples drawn from practice.

The Passionate Technique: Strategic Psychodrama with Individuals, Families and Groups (A. Williams), London: Routledge, 1989.

An overview of psychodrama which is then re-presented in terms of systems theory and strategic therapy.

Psychodrama: Inspiration and Technique (P. Holmes and M. Karp, eds), London: Routledge, 1991.

Psychodrama psychotherapists describe their work with a variety of client groups: 'This book describes how the boundaries of psychotherapy can be creatively stretched by the inspired use of technique, within the method of psychodrama and by the use of other theories, including ideas from psychoanalysis.'

Psychodrama Since Moreno: Innovations in Theory and Practice (P. Holmes, M. Karp and M. Watson, eds), London: Routledge, 1994.

The contributors are pre-eminent psychodramatists from many countries who address the developments in psychodrama since the death of Moreno.

REFERENCES

Aronson, M.L. (1991) Integrating Moreno's psychodrama and psychoanalytic group therapy. *Journal of Group Psychotherapy, Psychodrama and Sociometry*, 42: 199–203.

Badaines, A. (1988) Psychodrama. In J. Rowan and W. Dryden (eds), *Innovative Therapy in Britain*. Milton Keynes: Open University Press.

Bannister, A. (1991) Learning to live again: psychodramatic techniques with sexually abused young people. In P. Holmes and M. Karp (eds) *Psychodrama: Inspiration and Technique*. London: Routledge.

Ben-David, S. (1992) Influence, leadership, and desirability in psychotherapeutic groups. *Journal of Group Psychotherapy, Psychodrama and Sociometry*, 45: 17–23.

Blake, R.R. and McCanse, A.A. (1989) The rediscovery of sociometry. *Journal of Group Psychotherapy, Psychodrama and Sociometry*, 42 (3): 148–165.

Blatner, A. (1971) *Acting-in: Practical Applications of Psychodramatic Methods*. New York: Springer.

Blatner, A. (1997) *Acting-in: Practical Applications of Psychodramatic Methods*, 3rd edn. London: Free Association Books.

Blatner, A. (1995) *Psychodramatic Methods in Psychotherapy*. http://www.mhsource.com/edu/psytimes/p950520.html

Blatner, A. with Blatner, A. (1988) *Foundations of Psychodrama: History, Theory and Practice*, 3rd edn. New York: Springer.

Bloch, S. (1988) Research in group psychotherapy. In M. Aveline and W. Dryden (eds), *Group Therapy in Britain*. Milton Keynes: Open University Press.

Boal, A. (1979) *Theatre of the Oppressed*. London: Pluto.

Bohart, A.C. (1996) Experiencing, knowing, and change. In R. Hutterer, G. Pawlowsky, P.F. Schmid and R. Stipsits (eds), *Client-Centered and Experiential Psychotherapy: a Paradigm in Motion*. Frankfurt-am-Main: Peter Lang.

Bradbury, S. (1995a) That illusory hotbed of change. *Journal of the British Psychodrama Association*, 10 (2): 13–24.

Bradbury, S. (1995b) What does psychodrama do? Using the repertory grid to measure change. *British Journal of Psychodrama and Sociodrama*, 10 (1): 19–26.

Bustos, D.M. (1994) Wings and roots. In P. Holmes, M. Karp and M. Watson (eds), *Psychodrama since Moreno: Innovations in Theory and Practice*. London: Routledge.

Carlson-Sabelli, L., Sabelli, H. and Hale, A.E. (1994) Sociometry and sociodynamics. In P. Holmes, M. Karp and M. Watson (eds), *Psychodrama since Moreno: Innovations in Theory and Practice*. London: Routledge.

Casson, J. (1997a) The therapeusis of the audience. In S. Jennings (ed.), *Dramatherapy Theory and Practice*, Volume 3. London: Routledge.

Casson, J. (1997b) Psychodrama and individual psychotherapy. *British Journal of Psychodrama and Sociodrama*, 12 (1 & 2): 3–20.

Clayton, G.M. (1988) Psychodrama in Australia and New Zealand. *Journal of Group Psychotherapy, Psychodrama and Sociometry*, 41 (2): 63–76.

Coombes, S. (1991) Trusting the method. *Journal of the British Psychodrama Association*, 6 (2): 19–47.

Corey, G. (1994) *Theory and Practice of Group Counselling*, 4th edn. Pacific Grove, CA: Brooks–Cole.

Corti, P. and Casson, J. (1990) Dramatherapy into psychodrama: an account of a therapy group for women survivors of sexual abuse. *Journal of the British Psychodrama Association*, 5 (2): 37–53.

Costa, J. and Walsh, S. (1991) A psychodrama group for professional clinicians. *Journal of the British Psychodrama Association*, 6 (1): 24–37.

Drew, N. (1993) Re-enactment interviewing: a methodology for phenomenological research. *IMAGE: Journal of Nursing Scholarship*, 25 (4): 345–351.

Fox, J. (1995) *Acts of Service: Spontaneity, Commitment, Tradition in the Nonscripted Theater*. New Paltz, NY: Tusitala.

Goble, J. (1990) Didactic psychodrama and sociodrama. *Nurse Education Today*, 10: 457–464.

Hare, A.P. and Hare, J.R. (1996) *J.L. Moreno*. London: Sage.

Hare, J.R. (1988) Psychodrama in Israel. *Journal of Group Psychotherapy, Psychodrama and Sociometry*, 41 (2): 51–58.

Hawkins, P. (1988) A phenomenological psychodrama workshop. In P. Reason (ed.), *Human Inquiry in Action: Developments in New Paradigm Research*. London: Sage.

Holmes, P. (1991) Classical psychodrama: an overview. In P. Holmes and M. Karp (eds), *Psychodrama: Inspiration and Technique*. London: Routledge.

Holmes, P. (1992) *The Inner World Outside: Object Relations Theory and Psychodrama*. London: Routledge.

Holmes, P. (1995) How I assess for psychodrama groups or 'Would you like a cup of tea? In C. Mace (ed.), *The Art and Science of Assessment in Psychotherapy*. London: Routledge.

Honig, A.M. (1991) Psychotherapy with command hallucinations in chronic schizophrenia: the use of action techniques within a surrogate family setting. *Journal of Group Psychotherapy, Psychodrama and Sociometry*, 44 (1): 3–18.

Jay, S. (1992) Eating feelings: working with women who have bulimia. *Journal of the British Psychodrama Association*, 7 (2): 5–18.

Jefferies, J. (1991) What we are doing here is defusing bombs. In P. Holmes and M. Karp (eds), *Psychodrama: Inspiration and Technique*. London: Routledge.

Jones, P. (1996) *Drama as Therapy: Theatre as Living*. London: Routledge.

Kane, R. (1992) The potential abuses, limitations and negative effects of classical psychodramatic techniques in group counselling. *Journal of the British*

Psychodrama Association, 7 (2): 39–48 (Reprinted from the *Journal of Group Psychotherapy, Psychodrama and Sociometry*, 44 (2): 181–189).

Karp, M. (1988) Psychodrama in Britain: prophecy and legacy. *Journal of Group Psychotherapy, Psychodrama and Sociometry*, 41 (2): 45–50.

Karp, M. (1991) Psychodrama and piccalilli: residential treatment of a sexually abused adult. In P. Holmes and M. Karp (eds), *Psychodrama: Inspiration and Technique*. London: Routledge.

Karp, M. (1994) The river of freedom. In P. Holmes, M. Karp and M. Watson (eds), *Psychodrama since Moreno: Innovations in Theory and Practice*. London: Routledge.

Karp, M. (1995) An introduction to psychodrama. *Counselling*, 6 (4): 294–298.

Kellerman, P.F. (1985) Participants' perception of therapeutic factors in psychodrama. *Group Psychotherapy, Psychodrama and Sociometry*, 38: 123–132.

Kellerman, P.F. (1987a) A proposed definition of psychodrama. *Journal of Group Psychotherapy, Psychodrama and Sociometry*, 40 (2): 76–80.

Kellerman, P.F. (1987b) Psychodrama participants' perception of therapeutic factors. *Small Group Behavior*, 18: 408–419.

Kellerman, P.F. (1992) *Focus on Psychodrama: the Therapeutic Aspects of Psychodrama*. London: Jessica Kingsley.

Langley, D. (1994) The professional psychodrama psychotherapist. *British Journal of Psychodrama and Sociodrama*, 9 (1): 5–17.

Luxmore, N. (1995) Vignettes. *British Journal of Psychodrama and Sociodrama*, 10 (2): 5–17.

Marineau, R.F. (1989) *Jacob Levy Moreno 1889–1974: Father of Psychodrama, Sociodrama and Group Psychotherapy*. London: Tavistock/Routledge.

Marineau, R.F. (1994) The cradles of Moreno's contributions. In P. Holmes, M. Karp and M. Watson (eds), *Psychodrama since Moreno: Innovations in Theory and Practice*. London: Routledge.

McLeod, J. (1994) *Doing Counselling Research*. London: Sage.

Mearns, D. and Thorne, B. (1988) *Person-Centred Counselling in Action*. London: Sage.

Mendelson, P. (1989) The sociometric vision. *Journal of Group Psychotherapy, Psychodrama and Sociometry*, 42 (3): 138–147.

Moreno, J.D. (1994) Psychodramatic moral philosophy and ethics. In P. Holmes, M. Karp and M. Watson (eds), *Psychodrama since Moreno: Innovations in Theory and Practice*. London: Routledge.

Moreno, J.L. (1953) *Who Shall Survive?* New York: Beacon House.

Moreno, J.L. (1968) The validity of psychodrama. *Group Psychotherapy*, 21: 3.

Moreno, J.L. (1985) *Psychodrama*, Volume 1, 4th edn. Ambler, PA: Beacon House.

Moreno, J.L. and Moreno, Z.T. (1975) *Psychodrama*, Volume III: *Action Therapy and Principles of Practice*. Beacon, NY: Beacon House.

Moreno, Z.T. (1989) Psychodrama, role theory, and the concept of the social atom. *Journal of Group Psychotherapy, Psychodrama and Sociometry*, 42 (3): 178–187.

Nolte, J. (1989) Remembering J.L. Moreno. *Journal of Group Psychotherapy, Psychodrama and Sociodrama*, 42 (3): 129–137.

Orlinsky, D.E. and Howard, K.I. (1978) The relation of process to outcome in psychotherapy. In S.L. Garfield and A.E. Bergin (eds), *Handbook of Psychotherapy and Behaviour Change: an Empirical Analysis*, 2nd edn. New York: Wiley.

Özbay, H., Göka, E., Öztürk, E., Güngör, S. and Hincal, G. (1993) Therapeutic factors in an adolescent psychodrama group. *Journal of Group Psychotherapy, Psychodrama and Sociometry*, 46 (1): 3–11.

Pitzele, M.S. (1992) Moreno's chorus: the audience in psychodrama. *Journal of the British Psychodrama Association*, 7 (1): 5–8 (Reprinted from *Group Psychotherapy and Psychodrama*, 33, 1980).

Reason, P. and Rowan, J. (1981) *Human Inquiry: a Sourcebook of New Paradigm Research*. Chichester: Wiley.

Rogers, C.R. (1957) The necessary and sufficient of therapeutic personality change. *Journal of Consulting Psychology*, 21: 95–103.

Rogers, C.R. (1970) *Carl Rogers on Encounter Groups*. New York: Harper and Row.

Ruscombe-King, G. (1991) Hide and seek: the psychodramatist and the alcoholic. In P. Holmes and M. Karp (eds), *Psychodrama: Inspiration and Technique*. London: Routledge.

Rustin, T.A. and Olsson, P.A. (1993) Sobriety shop – a variation on magic shop for addiction treatment patients. *Journal of Group Psychotherapy, Psychodrama and Sociometry*, 46 (1): 12–22.

Sacks, J.M., Bilaniuk, M.-T. and Gendron, J.M. (1995) *Bibliography of Psychodrama*. New York: Psychodrama Center of New York.

Schutzenberger, A.A. (1991) The drama of the seriously ill patient: fifteen years' experience of psychodrama and cancer. In P. Holmes and M. Karp (eds), *Psychodrama Inspiration and Technique*. London: Routledge.

Sprague, K. (1991) Everybody's a somebody: action methods for young people with severe learning difficulties. In P. Holmes and M. Karp (eds), *Psychodrama: Inspiration and Technique*. London: Routledge.

Sprague, K. (1994) Stepping into the cosmos with our feet on the ground. In P. Holmes, M. Karp and M. Watson (eds), *Psychodrama since Moreno: Innovations in Theory and Practice*. London: Routledge.

Stallone, T.M. (1993) The effects of psychodrama on inmates within a structured residential behavior modification program. *Journal of Group Psychotherapy, Psychodrama and Sociometry*, 46 (1): 24–31.

Stein, M.B. and Callahan, M.L. (1982) The use of psychodrama in individual psychotherapy. *Journal of Group Psychotherapy, Psychodrama and Sociometry*, 35 (3): 118–129.

Tantum, D. (1995) Why assess? In C. Mace (ed.), *The Art and Science of Assessment in Psychotherapy*. London: Routledge.

Torres, A.R. (1998) Some remarks on psychodrama research. At http://members.tripod.com/~portaroma/psychodrama.html

VanderMay, J. and Peake, T. (1980) Psychodrama as a psychotherapy supervision technique. *Group Psychotherapy, Psychodrama and Sociometry*, 33 (1): 25–32.

Wilkins, P. (1993) Psychodrama: a vehicle for self-integration. *Journal of the British Psychodrama Association*, 8 (1): 5–17.

Wilkins, P. (1994a) Can psychodrama be 'person-centred'? *Person Centred Practice*, 2 (2): 14–18.

Wilkins, P. (1994b) The person centred approach to psychodrama. *British Journal of Psychodrama and Sociodrama*, 9 (2): 37–48.

Wilkins, P. (1995) A creative therapies model for the group supervision of counsellors. *British Journal of Guidance and Counselling*, 23 (2): 245–257.

Wilkins, P. (1997a) Psychodrama and research. *British Journal of Psychodrama and Sociodrama*, 12 (1 & 2): 44–61.

Wilkins, P. (1997b) *Personal and Professional Development for Counsellors*. London: Sage.

Williams, A. (1989) *The Passionate Technique: Strategic Psychodrama with Individuals, Families, and Groups*. London: Routledge.

Williams, A. (1991) *Forbidden Agendas: Strategic Action in Groups*. London: Routledge.

INDEX